Praise for
Can You Help Me Give a Sh*t?

"Engaging and enlightening."

- *Kirkus Reviews*

"A compelling read for educators, parents, and anyone invested in the future of education"

- *BookView Review*

"Essential reading for anyone committed to improving a teen's educational experience"

- *Literary Titan*, Gold Award Winner

"Concrete, thought-provoking insights about ... how educators, families, and teens can collaborate to make learning more meaningful"

- *Midwest Book Reviews*

"An undeniably useful guide to recognizing how teenagers from varying backgrounds are faring in today's world."

- *Independent Book Review*

"This important book helps you understand more about what's going on with the motivations, behaviors, and frustrations of teens in school and how to help them feel like they matter."

- Scott Barry Kaufman, PhD, cognitive scientist, author, and host of *The Psychology Podcast*

"...a game-changer in education .... As a higher education professional, I find it indispensable."

- Glenn Smith, Asst. Director, Berkley Achievement Scholarship Program at NYU

"This must-read book makes it easy to empathize with so many teens and young adults who find it hard or impossible to stay motivated in school, and what parents and educators of all types can do to help them. I highly recommend it!"

- Jared Kallen, M.S. Ed, Founder and Director of
Action Pact Coaching

"Igniting teen motivation is a big issue for adult development, life and career success.... This book is a rich and honest depiction of what teens are truly experiencing."

- Sarabeth Berk Bickerton, PhD, author of
More Than My Title

"As former head of People Development at Google, I see great value in helping young people develop the ability to understand and catalyze their own motivation. I have no doubt this will help them land and excel more smoothly in their careers."

- Karen May, PhD, Former VP of People Development,
Google

"One of the most refreshing reads on an essential topic.... This book demonstrates the practical and meaningful solutions that arise when researchers honor lived experience."

- Leah Mazzola, PhD, Founder/CEO of Youth
Coaching Institute

Can You Help Me Give a Sh*t?

Unlocking Teen Motivation in School and Life.

Rebecca R Block, PhD & Grace L Edwards

atmosphere press

To my mom, who tried hard to understand me when I was a teen and who never got to see how much her thoughtful listening, deep care, and fantastic sense of humor continue to inspire me as an adult. And to my sons, who inspire, exhaust, and exhilarate me every day—sometimes all in the same moment. - B.B.

To my father, who understood me as a child; my mother, who understood me as an adult; and my siblings, who keep me grounded and advocate for me. To my family, who support me in my journey of education, independence, and identity. - G.E.

Authors' Note

This book draws from observations and informal conversations with young people and parents that took place over the last five years and specifically cites formal interviews with 19 young people, aged 15-22, who we spoke with between the fall of 2021 and the summer of 2022. We conducted interviews live over video calls or in person and included young people from across the United States (see the list of interviewees in the Resources chapter for more details). With the exception of two students, Grace (the first interviewee, turned co-author) and Connor (an 18-year-old who had already spoken in several public forums about student voice), all other interviewees' names and identifying details have been changed to protect their privacy.

Contents

"People are fulfilled to the extent that they create their world."

- Paulo Freire, *Pedagogy of the Oppressed*

"When you understand someone's suffering, that's the best gift you can give that person. Understanding is love itself. Understanding is love's other name. If you don't understand, you can't love."

- Thich Nhat Hanh, *How to Love*

Introduction

In New Mexico, a high school study-skills teacher asks her sophomores and juniors to write down what they want to get out of her class. One writes, "Can you help me give a shit about school? I want to, but I just don't know how."

In Pennsylvania, a junior questions her mom about the usefulness of school. "What's the point of these classes? Why does it matter if I learn this stuff?" Her mom, frustrated, replies, "Ask your teachers; they should be able to tell you why it matters."

In North Carolina, a senior asks his math tutor why he has to learn Algebra II to graduate high school. The tutor googles what jobs use advanced algebra skills—and is startled to realize only six percent of jobs do. "It helps with logical thinking," she says, hoping she's right.

In New Jersey, a father acknowledges that his sophomore is doing "just fine" academically. "But it just seems to be about compliance," he opines. "I don't care if he gets all 'A's; I want him to learn how to learn, and it doesn't seem like school is teaching him that."

In Florida, a soon-to-be freshman questions whether he wants to do the International Baccalaureate (IB) program, a rigorous four-year course of study that is available at his high school. He's done well in his classes in middle school but doesn't have a particularly strong academic drive. His mother worries IB could be too much pressure—she's read the stories of how teens are increasingly stressed out and overwhelmed—but also worries he would get bored and even more disinterested without a challenging academic curriculum. "I don't know what to encourage him to do, honestly," she confides.

Online, a parent asks a "parenting of teens" Facebook group why their kid is so apathetic about school. "Is there something wrong with them? Is this just the effects of COVID lingering? Or is something else going on?" Another parent responds that her son became so miserable in high school he basically withdrew to the basement of their house. "He graduated six months ago, but he still doesn't know what's next. I've tried to get him to see a range of options, different kinds of colleges, work, service—I don't know if I'm pushing too hard or not enough."

If any of these stories ring true, you're not alone. While it's nothing new for students—especially teens—to dislike school, the cumulative effects of the last few years (COVID lockdowns, teacher and student burnout, staffing shortages, political tensions, rapid technological change, and the ever-increasing cost of college) have made school somehow feel both highly stressful *and* mostly irrelevant to many students, families, and educators.

For the lucky students, school only sucks occasionally. For the unlucky, it's a miserable experience. Every. Single. Day. Though it may be most visible in the students who are struggling academically or in those who are visibly depressed, withdrawn, or anxious, even the students we spoke with who were academically successful and not struggling with their mental health felt like school was very rarely about engaged *learning* and far more often about simply performing well enough to either get by or meet expectations.

This aimlessness and suffering is not due to a lack of effort, from legislators all the way to individual students:

- Legislators passed No Child Left Behind decades ago, revised it with the Every Student Succeeds Act in 2015, and then made further efforts with federal COVID-19 recovery funds beginning in 2020.

- Administrators and school boards put in extra hours to navigate new initiatives, like those coming from federal or state mandates,[1] while responding to emergent crises, like staffing and teacher shortages and student mental health needs.

- Teachers undergo days of new professional development every year on the latest teaching methods and curriculum, from teaching "new math" to cultural competency, and most put in extra hours to try to make that new material relevant and engaging for their students.

- Parents drag themselves to late-night, marathon school board meetings and help their kids navigate situations with school, work, and, for many, the overwhelming college admission process, plus the mix of texts, emails, robocalls, apps, and school software tools like Schoology, PowerSchools, Classdojo, and more.

- Students, meanwhile, juggle everything from the challenges of early start times to extracurriculars, homework, multiple software platforms, and difficult and/or boring classes. They do this while in the midst of massive brain- and identity developments that increase the stakes when navigating shifts in romantic interests, friend groups, social media norms, local and international politics, and decisions about what to do with their lives after high school.

No one has it easy in this equation. And no wonder—we want school to accomplish a *lot*. School should be equitable and safe, physically and psychologically. This is a crucial foundation, yet it remains out of reach for many, especially for schools with the least resources and for students who are furthest from the mainstream. On top of that, school should prepare young people for college, work, and citizenship despite an increasing rate of change in technology and society that makes it harder and harder to predict what skills will actually be useful even five years down the road. School should challenge and set high expectations—but also be differentiated and provide the right support for each student's abilities and goals. And somehow, school should do all this affordably, as a public system paid for by our tax dollars.

Whew. It's not surprising that so many adults and young people alternate between hair-pulling stress and overwhelmed apathy when we think about school, our families, and the future.

So Then, What Can We Do About It?

There is plenty already written about how school should and could work to solve all the problems mentioned above. We're not trying to add to that impressive collection. Instead, this book is intended to help the parents and educators who are in the thick of it *right now*, those who are trying to figure out how to help teens navigate the next few months or years. This book is focused on how adults and teens can engage as co-pilots in the process of steering the experience of school (especially high school) away from overwhelm, disempowerment, and apathy and towards an experience where both parents and teens can feel connected and capable.

Why does feeling connected and capable matter? For anyone to navigate any lasting, challenging situation—and school certainly qualifies—they have to have sustained motivation. Not the quick hits of panic that give a boost to cram for a test or stuff yet one more thing into an overfull day. Not the slowly draining motivation that can come from people pleasing and meeting other people's expectations. But the kind of motivation to learn, act, and take responsible risks that gives energy in both the short and long term, the kind that's more like stringing together several nights of good sleep than downing a few shots of espresso.

Both of us, Becca and Grace, have different experiences that have sparked our interest in better understanding what can be done to support students being genuinely engaged and motivated in their learning. For me,[2] Becca, this interest started when working as a college professor teaching introductory writing classes. I noticed that students were arriving to my first-year writing courses completely checked out. They were so used to feeling no sense of interest or passion for their learning that they just looked at me, annoyed, when I told them they could study and write about any subject they wished in whatever writing form was meaningful to their career or personal goals. They asked me, over and over again, to please just tell them what I wanted them to write about and how they should write it so they could pass the class. I realized that if I wanted to help students (including my own kids) thrive rather than just scrape by, I needed to (1) build my understanding of positive youth development and (2) start doing things to help students *before* they got to college. That led me to leave my tenured position and begin working for organizations that support K-12, where I use my research skills to more deeply understand young people and education and then apply those learnings to help evaluate and design effective programs for young people.

Additionally, as my kids grew, I talked with more and more parents and saw how many of us were struggling to know how to best support our kids in school, especially as they approached high school. I found plenty of books that focused on sharing everything the experts had to say, but student voices usually played a very small part in these books. My experiences as a parent, educator, evaluator, and designer, as well as others' research on positive youth development, have taught me that deeply listening to those who are experiencing the problem—in this case, young people themselves—is the crucial first step to building lasting solutions. We can't assume we know what someone else is really struggling with, even (perhaps especially) when it's our own kid. So, I started talking to young people, informally at first, asking them about their school experiences, what they hated, what they liked, what they hoped for. Whenever I would casually mention something from one of these conversations to another parent, their eyes would light up, and they would say things like, "So, it's not just my kid?" or "I have to share that idea with my high schooler." Because I couldn't find enough good resources that put students' experiences at the center, I decided to start one and began conducting more formal interviews with young people across the country.

For Grace, this interest was catalyzed by what turned out to be a harsh transition from high school to university. In high school, she had been involved in a few student activist organizations, and by virtue of being a student journalist, she had been encouraged by how her voice, and other students' voices, could be used to educate and connect people with the support of the adults around her. She came to university hoping to find similar spheres of support to help her pursue her academic and career interests. However, her prestigious university was not as supportive as she had expected. She wondered why it was so difficult to connect with her peers and some of her teachers and find the same motivation that she had towards high school with college. She wanted to feel reassured that she could still enjoy school and grow as a student, as she had previously. When I approached her as a potential interviewee for the book, she was initially just willing to share her stories about the differences in her high school and college experiences in the hopes of helping parents understand her generation better and be able to better support their children. When I asked her if, given her interest and background in student journalism, she wanted to become my coauthor, she said yes. "I thought it would be a fun opportunity to build my writing experience, in addition to uplifting student's voices in the same way my voice was elevated in high school. As I talked with other students, I felt connected, encouraged by their stories, and it made me feel less alone, and I noticed the students we spoke to also felt less alone in their experiences." In the process, Grace said, "I saw how all our stories would, hopefully, give parents and young people alike more ideas on how to make their school experiences better."

We interviewed young people from all over the country, mostly high schoolers but some college and university students, so they could talk about the differences between high school and after. When we asked students to describe their most and least engaging learning experiences, several themes emerged—themes that, unsurprisingly, match existing decades of literature about what it takes for humans to sustain motivation in any context, not just school. This kind of motivation is called "autonomous motivation" in psychological literature, and it involves a powerful mix of intrinsic motivation with meaningful extrinsic motivation.[3] To sustain this kind of motivation, we need to feel like we have (or can build) the abilities we need to succeed at the goal at hand, that we belong with people who can help us achieve it, and that we can make meaningful choices about both what we're pursuing and how we get there. In that class in New Mexico, where the student asked how to give a shit about high school, her teacher responded to her student's request by introducing these elements as "the ABCs of motivation: ability, belonging, and choices." In psychological research, these are referred to as competence, relatedness, and autonomy,[4] but since we noticed students and parents alike found the ABC mnemonic easier to remember, that's what we use throughout the book.

That school in New Mexico isn't the only one where students are wondering if it's possible to give a shit about school. Nationwide, even before the pandemic, only about one-third of high schoolers felt engaged in school.[5] But as one of our interviewees discussed, while it may look like students are apathetic, it's really hard not to care, on some level, about something you're spending most of your time doing. Young people *want* to care about school but retreat into apathy when they don't see good ways to shape their school experience into one that's meaningful to them. And regardless of whether you're familiar with the decades of research on the topic, it's obvious on its face: who could maintain the energy to keep trying and caring if they feel like they lack the ability to succeed at what they're being asked to do? If they don't feel like they belong in their school and classes? If they lack meaningful choices about what they're being asked to learn and how they learn it and see no evidence that the requirements they're told to push through will be relevant for their present *or* their future? It's not surprising that every story students shared with us where they described being engaged in their learning had all three of those elements (ability, belonging, and choice) present—and every story of disengagement had at least one, if not all three, missing.

In order to be good co-pilots in charting the way through a better school experience, however, it's not enough for adults and teens to just know what makes it possible to sustain motivation and what gets in the way of it lasting. It's not hard to imagine what would happen if a parent walked up to their teenager and said, "Hey, so you just need to feel like you can do what they're asking you to do, feel like you have some decent relationships with at least a few of your teachers and peers, and also feel like you got to make some real choices (and see why the requirements you can't make choices around are useful). So . . . what's missing? Let's figure out how to get that!"

Just for fun, I actually tried saying that to my middle schooler. His response was to wrinkle his forehead, roll his eyes, and mutter, "Mom, you're *so weird.*"

As any adult who spends time with teens has probably

learned the hard way, approaching them with something to tell them that you think they would benefit from knowing almost never turns out well, no matter how well-intentioned. Approaching them with a genuine interest in listening to understand, however—not to judge, or to catch them out, or to insert an anecdote—tends to go better. Particularly if you haven't inadvertently done bait-and-switch conversational tactics too many times already, the kind that starts off with good intentions of just asking them about something but goes sideways quickly.

The one I am most guilty of as a parent usually goes like this:

Me: "How was school today?"

My son: "Fine, but I have too much homework."

Me: "Wait, then why were you watching TV before dinner if you still have homework to do?!"

Oops. It's hard to listen without switching into judging and directing when something concerns us, especially for parents who feel responsible for successfully launching their kids into adulthood. But it's vital. And it helps to have practice. That's one reason this book is packed with far more student stories than research summaries and expert opinions (though we have those, too, for those who want to dig more). To understand, we have to listen deeply. To listen deeply, we have to set aside our own fear and agenda, at least for a little while (don't worry, you can pick it up again when you're chatting with a co-parent or texting with your friends). To set aside our fears and agendas takes practice in noticing when they're coming up. So, if while reading the stories here, you find yourself feeling that flash or fear or urge to fix, just notice what triggered it. Then you can be on the lookout for that trigger when it counts, when you're listening to your own kid.

The other reason this book is driven by student stories is because those stories offer insight, hope, and real-world examples. These examples can both help adults and students feel less alone in their struggles, as well as offer ideas on what students and adults could try to see if what helped another young person might help them too. This book is intended to help any adult—parents, guardians, educators, counselors, or other caretakers—who is seeking ideas on how to understand and support teens who'd like school to suck less. We've organized it into themed, approachable stories so it's easy to jump to the chapters most relevant to you and to share relevant sections with young people directly. Many of our interviewees really appreciated learning about the experiences of other young people from around the country, so we wanted to make it easy for you to share them, too.

So, for school to be more engaging, students need to feel like they have the abilities, belonging, and choices to stay motivated. That means they need to be in the driver's seat, with the adults who care about them serving as the kind of front-seat passenger who helps them navigate tricky roads rather than the kind who pumps imaginary brakes and sucks in panicked breaths at every turn.

To play that role, adults need to listen to students deeply, build solutions *with* them rather than *for* them, and help them connect with others and expand their sense of what's possible. That's why each chapter concludes with specific ideas of what adults can do to help build the sense of ability, belonging, or choices those stories illustrate: to make it easier to take action from this deepened understanding. And that's why the first part of this book focuses on belonging—because it's not possible to help young people see their abilities, build new ones, make choices, and perceive relevance without first having a mutually trusting and authentic relationship.[6]

While the idea of stepping from the driver's seat to the passenger's seat to let students lead the way has the potential to make parents' lives less overwhelming and is far more likely to set young people up for both immediate engagement and later success in adulthood, it's easier said than done.[7] There is a *lot* of social pressure and fear driving you to stay hyper-vigilant and in (attempted) control of kids' lives, even if you may sense you aren't helping them by doing that. Educators and administrators are also pressured to meet community and legislative expectations, measured by student test scores and college acceptance rates rather than in resilience and later success.[8]

In other words, while the principle of stepping back and supporting young people in taking the lead is simple, it's hard to practice. Especially because supporting young people in developing this kind of agency[9] doesn't happen overnight—even if all parents and schools suddenly started offering genuine opportunities for student choice tomorrow, many teens would respond to that opportunity with ongoing cynicism, apathy, or simple confusion. It's necessary, but not sufficient, to give students *actual* opportunities to foster belonging, exercise their abilities, and make meaningful choices, but we can't force young people to immediately *feel* their abilities, sense of belonging, and choices are genuine.

No one can make someone else have lasting motivation, especially not in just a few experiences or without the scaffolding to grow the mindsets and skills needed to both *feel* and *be* connected, capable, and focused. It's a journey, and like all good journeys, you'll be better equipped for the ride if you don't expect it to flash by in a blink. So, give yourself and the young people you care about the gift of time. Even if all that changes initially is that you find it easier to understand what they might be experiencing. Just that, as the Thich Nhat Hahn quote at the start of the book reminds us, is a significant gift to give anyone.

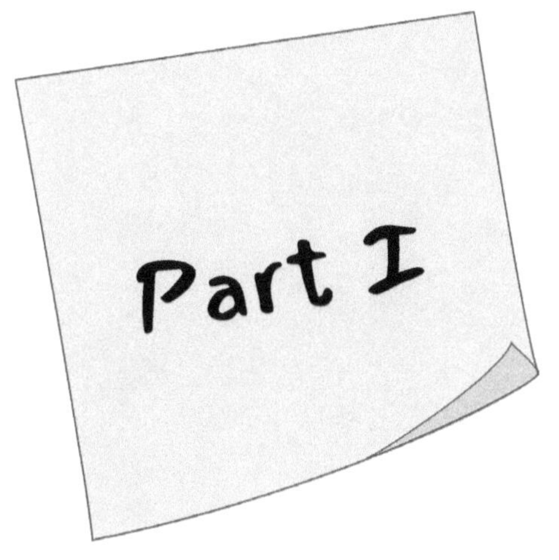

Belonging Lays the Foundation for Lasting Motivation

1

Freedom With Boundaries

How Families Can Support Learning

"This is something I didn't really understand for a long time, but I think being a teenager is just really hard. Even if you don't have those big sob-story reasons why you're doing poorly in school. I think sometimes people like to dig for that. 'Why are they struggling in school? Why are their grades falling? Why are they depressed?' Right? Even if you don't have a clear-cut answer, it's really hard growing up and dealing with all these emotions, dealing with parents, dealing with finding friends, dealing with not having friends, insecurity—those emotions are hard to deal with, especially when you're growing up and learning how to deal with them for the first time. And I think compassion without needing a reason . . . would be definitely nice to have from other people and adults. Like that genuine care, even if, you know, someone didn't die, even if you don't have a big reason. I think that is important. Growing up is hard. . . . I think if someone had just sat down with me and asked me, genuinely, how I'm doing and what was going on, especially during my sophomore and junior year, it would have changed some things for me."

- Melanie

Setting Clear and Healthy Expectations

When reading parenting books, it's common to come across the advice to be "authoritative" (clear, firm, and consistent) rather than "authoritarian" (controlling and rigid) or "permissive" (no rules, no consistency, anything goes).[10] It's easy to imagine expectations as a continuum and see why we all (young people and adults both!) want a balance between just enough structure to create stability and trust but not so much that we stifle communication and independence. But in practice, striking that balance can be tricky. Below are the stories students shared with us of examples when their families managed to find that balance, and when they missed the mark.

Goose: "Whatever I do now is good enough."

Goose, a high school senior at a suburban public school in the Northeast, was born in America, but her parents and older brother immigrated here from Brazil not long before her birth. She described herself as "eccentric" and as someone who was a bit "goth" and had niche interests; she also talked about how she felt like she struggled sometimes with depression and anxiety. She also described the school district she lived in as fairly wealthy and said she often felt out of place having two immigrant parents from South America who didn't have the kind of high-income jobs many of her peers' parents had.

For Goose, her family's immigration status meant expectations around schooling and success felt complicated:

When you think of first-generation students, I feel like you always hear about how successful and great some of these people are and how they go off to Harvard, blah, blah, blah. And it makes it hard kind of for me because I want to be that person . . . but I'm kind of, like, I wouldn't say I'm average, but that's just not my experience right now. And so, also considering that and considering that I want to make [my parents] proud, but I also want to make myself and others proud . . . my mom picked me up on the last day of school, and she was crying, and she said, "My job with you is done. You're educated; you went to high school." So, whatever I do now is good enough. But it's just like, what now?

Goose appreciates that her parents' expectation was simply that she successfully complete high school and that her mom was proud of her for doing exactly that. But she also feels the rub between this and the broader cultural expectations that pressure her into wanting to make her parents, and others, proud by aspiring to achieve *more*.

She described how this was different for her than for her older brother since he had been born outside the U.S. shortly before her family moved here:

His experience was very different. He didn't really feel motivated to do very well because, you know, after school, like paying for college and then potentially not being able to get a job because of his papers. And so, his experience was so different from mine that when I went into high school, I had no expectations of what he did. All I knew was that he was barely passing.

Because Goose's brother was fully aware that an investment in his education might not pay out financially due to the status of his immigration papers in this country, he saw no point in investing in school. This meant that Goose felt that "everything [she] did was just out of [her] own skill and just [her] working toward stuff" because her parents "offered [her] so much morally, but in terms of education, no," since their own educational background was so different.

These baseline expectations allowed Goose to focus on the areas in high school she was most interested in and be a self-identified "high achiever" in those specific areas for a simple reason: "I really like to learn." For example:

English has really been like the driving thing that keeps me going; I've always been really great in those courses ... there's so much to learn about that. It never really gets boring. And it just so happens that in the courses that I take that are honors, I do well because I have so much experience with it. So that's really like what I go after. When it came to math or science, I didn't push myself more than I needed to because I knew that wasn't going to help me.

In other words, because Goose's family simply expected her to graduate high school but didn't push her to be an overall academic high achiever, she was selective about where to put her efforts. She focused on areas where she felt both interest and success. This aligns with the meta-analysis of over 220,000 students done by self-determination theory researchers, who found that students driven by intrinsic motivation had positive short and long-term life outcomes, whereas those driven by extrinsic factors (like avoiding punishment or obtaining rewards) or by "ego-involved motives," did not.[11]

This difference contributes to the unhealthy levels of stress students in high-achieving schools often feel. The emphasis is on achieving high marks and impressive resumes across the board in pursuit of elusive rewards like admission to an Ivy League school, where the pressure cranks even higher to pursue the next big reward of high-paying jobs and high-profile professional networks. In the process, the motivation to learn becomes replaced by a motivation to *perform*, which is a speedy path to burnout. Goose was able to avoid this trap because of her parents' clear and reasonable expectations, which allowed her to discover a sustaining source of motivation to weather other challenges discussed in later chapters.

Caprielle: "My family, we highly value our education."

Often, expectations are conveyed simply as shared values within the family, as was the case for Caprielle. Caprielle described herself as a White 17-year-old junior who came from a divorced family, where she was raised solely by her single mother and two older sisters. She was completing her last two years of high school through a dual-enrollment program with her local community college and talked about how she approached a set of challenges she ran into earlier in her high school career:

I never let it affect my academics too much because I take too much pride in that stuff. Just because, like my sisters, we highly value our education because we grew up in an all-girl house-hold—a single mom raised me, and I have two older sisters. It's a very female empowerment-centered place. So, I always try to never let that stuff [outside circumstances] affect my grades because I know how important academics are for my future.

The downside of this orientation for Caprielle is the over-lap between being a people pleaser and being academically successful, especially for women:[12]

So, I've come from, again, a family that highly valued education because my mom always made it known that no one can ever take education away from you. Take the time to do it, and then you can do later things in life. I was raised with the view that education—along with happiness—should be the number-one priority, and I completely agree. I'm all for that. Especially after hearing about my mother's experience and lessons, I really want to learn from her challenges. So yeah, it's always just come easy to me to be a people pleaser. It's just kind of in my nature, but I'm definitely learning to value my own worth, and my own likes and interests, and not compromise myself for anyone, whether that be a fellow classmate or a future friend, or a teacher, or anyone.

The overlap between girls frequently being more inclined toward pleasing people, and therefore more inclined to do well in school, is sufficient material for a separate book in and of itself. Here, we call it out primarily to again indicate the tension between healthy and unhealthy expectations. Overall, Caprielle experiences her family's focus on education and academic achievement as a positive expectation that drives her to focus on areas she believes are the most important. Because that expectation wasn't for success at all costs—her family values happiness, as well—she was able to notice that sometimes focusing on her academics overlapped with an unhealthy habit of focusing on pleasing everyone around her rather than balancing between her needs and theirs. This balance of expectations in her family left space for her to become more mindful about how she pursues academic success.

Connor: "Don't get into trouble; let us know what's going on, and please do well."

Connor, an 18-year-old high school senior in a unique public dual-enrollment program in Kentucky, lived on a college campus several hours drive away from his parents. When we asked him to describe himself, he said, "I'm a White man, I'm gay, I'm cis, I'm a Kentuckian, I'm a scientist, [and] I'm a researcher in computer science, bioinformatics, and sociology; I want to improve communities. I want to find a way to use technology for good and to solve problems the world is facing both between global and local levels." He also laughed and said, "I might add as an addendum to that description, 'some of that may change.'"[13]

Connor was also one of the interviewees who talked the most in-depth about the ways he and his parents communicated about their expectations and his choices:[14]

So, they have an agenda for me. And the agenda for me is, "Don't get into trouble, let us know what's going on, and please do well." Those were the big things. It's just . . . "find your trajectory, and don't mess it up too bad. Like, don't get into prison, don't do illegal things, and we'll be fine." And . . . there were times in my life where I'm like, "I'm going to go out with friends until 3 a.m.," as long as they knew where I was, and they knew that I was going to do that, and I was back at 3 a.m., they didn't mind it. As long as I kept my word and I kept who I was, they were okay with it. Because they knew that if I was doing what I said I was doing, then there was no reason for them not to have trust and faith in me. There was no reason to assume that we were on different agendas or that we were on different wavelengths.

The overall impression we gathered was that, for Connor, the boundaries set by his parents were more like firm principles than rules, ones that relied on trust and open communication.

Of course, sometimes parents and teens do get "on different wavelengths," even in a strong relationship:

One time, I think in late middle school, early high school . . . I got involved with this user-testing platform, where I would test websites and products and look for different bugs and give user-experience questionnaires and stuff. And I was making some good money off of it. And I didn't tell my parents that I was actually doing it. . . . And so, when they did inevitably find out, it was very much just like, "Hey, buddy, whatcha doing over there?" And it came from a place of "I'm glad that you're doing this. And I'm glad that you found out about this. And the fact that you're looking to make money for yourself is good. And that tells us other things about what you want to do and how you want to spend your time. This is a good thing that you're looking for different pursuits. But it's not great that you didn't tell us about it. And it's not great that we didn't have a look at it first and that we didn't have that conversation. Because that breaks trust and that back-and-forth that we tend to have because you're lying by omission." And so that sort of sense of just being upfront about what's going on and . . . what I'm doing. And starting from that place of trust and assuming good faith. And assuming that we both have our best interests in mind. That's something that I think has been very implicit and something that's hard to do. But starting from that place of trust and that expectation of "I want you to do well, and I expect you to do well. And I'll intervene if I don't think that you are. But as long as you seem happy, and you seem to be on a path that is okay, to where it won't land you in prison, or it won't land you homeless, we're okay with that. Whatever works for you."

As Connor's story illustrates, it's not that he was a perfect child who never did anything that flagged concern from his parents (though we imagine that some parents reading this might be thinking, "I wish the thing my kid was sneaking was essentially a part-time job!"). However, his story makes it clear that this fairly expansive but still firm set of expectations required ongoing trust and communication from both Connor and his parents.

Grace asked Connor why he and his parents were able to approach each other in that open and communicative way. His answer:

I think early on, what helped a lot was the fact that when I was in school, I was fine. I was doing well in my classes; my teachers had good things to say about me. And so that was something that my parents were supportive of. And my parents didn't have the best educational career, as I've kind of alluded to, where they both dropped out of college; they weren't the best in high school. And in their home lives, both of them felt very locked down by their parents at times. Where my mom felt like she didn't have much control of her life, she felt a lot of pressure on her at all times throughout her childhood. Whereas my father felt like he had a bit too much at times and, at other times, felt like he had way too little. And so he was kind of flipping on this bipolar life-style of sometimes he could do whatever he wanted, and sometimes he was locked down for an undetermined amount of time.... And so, my parents both kind of came at parenting from a sense of, we want to make sure that you're doing well academically because we weren't able to do that. And so, we want to emphasize education as a way for you to be successful. And on top of that, we want you to have freedom and flexibility with oversight. We want to know what's going on, but what your own actions are are your own actions. And sometimes you need to deal with the consequences of that on your own, and we'll help out. But what you do with your own life is your own life. And while there should be oversight, having that freedom and being able to, say, go out with friends until 3 a.m., or work on a project for a long period of time, or do a certain program, or engage with a certain extracurricular activity. While there is the privilege inherent in that, starting from that place [of freedom with oversight], I think, really, really helped.

Connor's description of "freedom and flexibility with oversight" is, obviously, what informed the title of this chapter, as it's the best short description we encountered of the kind of approach that sets students up to build the kind of sustained motivation Deci, Ryan and the other psychological researchers discuss in the meta-analysis we referenced above, when sharing Goose's story. It's also what adolescent clinical psychologists recommend to parents to help their kids actually launch into adulthood. Adolescence is the time for this trial and error, for young people to practice independence before they can become truly independent.[15]

For example, even Connor's story about being caught sneaking user-testing work makes it clear that the way his parents responded to his boundary-crossing was both to reinforce the boundary *and* to talk about what it might reveal about his interests, about what might be motivating for him to continue to study and pursue over time. While some folks (young and not-as-young) are very clear on what their goals and interests are all the time, many of us aren't, and it requires a little detective work to determine what kind of work and activities can give us sufficient energy to sustain the motivation to do them over a longer period of time. These conversations aren't possible without the oversight that allows noticing what is arising that might be something to explore, nor without the freedom and flexibility to do that exploring.

Ava, Layla, Melanie, and Tuesday: Don't expect me to be someone I'm not.

As parents, we have to be careful that the way we set expectations doesn't convey a fundamental disapproval of who our kids are and what they're struggling with. Ava, a 17-year-old senior at a public high school in the Southeast, had attended both private and public schools in recent years, including, briefly, a boarding school (before COVID-19 lockdowns sent her back home). When we asked how she wanted to be described, she also shared, "I have four siblings. I'm the second oldest. My mom and dad are first-generation immigrants, so I'm a second-generation immigrant from Vietnam. I paint, and I'm third in the class at my school. I'm in many organizations. I'm Catholic [and] a first-generation college student, and I'll be attending [a well-known university in her state] in the fall." She saw herself as a high-performing student and noted that her parents "just expected" her to do well at school, and she said that basic expectation was fine.

However, when Ava tried to talk with her mom about some mental health challenges she was experiencing, her mother's expectations that she could just snap out of it were harmful. "I told my mom that I felt like I was [suicidal], and she said,

'You have a roof over your head, and food, and a great education; what more do you have to worry about?' So that was very damaging to my health."

Layla, a 19-year-old first year at a competitive university in the Northeast, described herself as Black, Muslim, bisexual, and someone who struggled sometimes with mental health issues. She had attended public school K-12 in the U.S., and her parents had immigrated to the U.S. from Egypt. She also had a disheartening experience when attempting to talk with her mom about her mental health. Like Ava, it seemed like her mom's expectations for how Layla should feel about her life just didn't align with how Layla actually felt, and the gap between those expectations and Layla's experience made communication challenging. "She does it consistently, where I tell her about my issues, and she's like, 'Well, you were just fine.' I was like, 'Yeah, but I was fine for about a month, which is true, a long time, but I'm still, it wasn't actually *fine*—[there were still] a lot of lows and a lot of highs.'" For Layla, who spoke to us a few months after pushing her way out of a depressive episode that had resulted in a suicide attempt, those highs and lows were a real reason for concern and one she wanted her parents to take seriously as well:

> *I came to talk to my parents. I had anxiety and depression. They viewed it as if I'm, I don't know how to explain it. Like it was a completely willing and conscious thing. . . . And they're just like, "Okay, then here are some options for help." And it's not things that I need, like psychiatric or therapist help; it's like, "Maybe you should study less." I can't study less. I'm not in an environment where I can, so I need to figure out how to cope, hopefully.*

It was very disheartening for Layla to feel like her parents couldn't understand why she was feeling the way she felt and why she needed the kind of support she was asking for.

For Layla, this was compounded by them not understanding the uniquely isolating feeling of "sometimes being the only Black girl in my engineering classes. Like I said, my parents just don't get it." This was part of a series of examples Layla shared from her school experiences that had left her feeling unsafe for being Black, Muslim, and female in a highly-ranked science program at a competitive university that had a primarily White student (and teacher) population. When she tried to talk to her parents about the added stress of being isolated in all these ways, however, their response was, "At least you're at [this competitive university]."

Melanie, an 18-year-old high school senior in the Northeast, described herself as a high-achieving student, an Asian American child of immigrant parents, and a queer woman. Melanie attributed some of the disconnects in her relationship with her parents to their different backgrounds. "So, I think, with my parents, there has always been kind of a cultural gap because they're immigrants. Like, I never was very emotionally connected to them. But that was, I think, exacerbated by [my mom's cancer treatments from eighth to eleventh grade]." During one summer, Melanie lived with an older sister while her mom underwent extensive cancer treatments in a large city several hours away from where they lived.

Melanie went on to describe a tension with her parents regarding her identity as a queer person; however, because Melanie's relationship with her parents was already emotionally disconnected, she noted that this particular tension didn't substantially change their relationship. "I would say my relationship with my parents has always been fine. Like, muted. Like, we didn't really talk much, but we didn't fight either. It was fine. I've never doubted their love for me. I know they've sacrificed a lot for me."

Though the year she was "forced to come out" due to her mother finding and reading her journals was a very challenging one for her whole family, specifically because of her parents' religious beliefs, she still thinks this description of their relationship applies overall. As Melanie put it:

They were concerned, especially within the context of the church . . . they've been as kind as they can be, but that difference in opinion is still there, and it's just made home tense at times. There were a couple months in there that were like, 'I don't want to be home.' I was out all the time, studying at the library . . . and I think it was definitely difficult, but I think I've gotten much better at communicating with people. Talking to, opening up, and that has been immensely helpful.

Melanie had already formed positive relationships with her teachers that were especially helpful for her; school had been her haven before when her mom was undergoing cancer treatments, and it remained that way during this new challenge.

When parents and children hold different values, regardless of whether it's because of cultural, religious, political, or generational differences, figuring out what it means to have a healthy set of clear expectations is more challenging. When we can ground our expectations in curiosity and care, such that our teens feel supported in who they are, we're more likely to succeed in helping them safely try, fail, and have the energy to try again. But that isn't always easy to do.[16] It's not hard to empathize with Ava, Layla, or Melanie's parents—they want what's best for their kids, the same as all parents do, and they were probably responding from worry and fear. Unfortunately, the effect was that Ava, Layla, and Melanie each felt some crucial part of their experience wasn't understood or accepted, and it dimmed their sense of connection with their parents.

Tuesday, an 18-year-old senior at a small public high school (about 400 students) in an inland state of the Northwest, described himself as biracial (White and Asian), trans, assigned female at birth, and someone who struggled with mental health issues triggered by bullying he experienced in school. He learned the hard way how much of an impact parental expectations could have on being able to feel like he belonged in school when he tried to come out as trans. As Tuesday put it, "My parents were really against my transition. And so, when I socially came out, they talked to the school board, and so they got the school board to continue to use she/her pronouns for me, despite me coming out to everybody." Learning took a back seat to just trying to make it through the school day unscathed, and Tuesday couldn't turn to his parents for support navigating this unwelcoming environment at school. The expectation coming from his parents and most of the adults in his school was to be someone other than himself, and it made school much harder.

Tuesday, Elena, and King: Sometimes parents should set expectations with the school itself.

While Tuesday's experience was negative, it showed him how much power parents could have in how students are treated at school. He had advice for other young people who, like him, were advocating for positive change of any kind in their schools. "If the school board wants to do nothing about it, and the teachers won't change, I would recommend talking to family [or], like, another adult . . . to be able to talk to the school board because I've noticed that the school board has been more willing to change when it's an adult talking to them." Parents and other caretakers have the opportunity to use their status in their communities to help young people advocate for their needs when they notice districts are unresponsive to students advocating on their own. For example, Elena said it would be great if adults could advocate to help push high-school start times later—in alignment with medical advice that's been around for over a decade—and get kids using lockers rather than being "zombie tortoises" around the hallways. As she put it, "I just remember feeling way too tired at way too young of an age and carrying around a backpack load. It was just not very healthy."

Of course, adult advocacy doesn't always succeed, but even when it doesn't, the effort is noticed and deeply cherished. King, a 15-year-old homeschool sophomore in the Northeast, described how he had been one of the few Black students in his primarily White and fairly wealthy public school district and had experienced multiple racially charged incidents throughout his public elementary and middle school education prior to switching to homeschooling. "Me leaving the school district was a real intervention because I felt like my parents knew that if they kept me in that school district, I was going to falter off the path or something bad was gonna happen to me. Because my mental health was not good." Prior to switching to homeschooling, however, his parents came in and talked with school administrators and teachers on multiple occasions, trying to address the ways he was being alienated and excluded, and King saw and deeply appreciated that advocacy. (Later chapters on peers and teachers discuss more about King's experiences that sparked his parents' involvement.)

Understanding School Systems and Options

Students don't necessarily *need* their parents and families to understand how their local schools work—but it can help when they do. Goose, for instance, talked about how having immigrant parents who hadn't participated in schools in the U.S. made it harder for her to figure out her options. On the flip side, students whose families did have a strong understanding of how their schools worked, and what options were open to students, described how that knowledge made it easier to navigate challenges in school and take advantage of opportunities they might have otherwise missed.

Avery: "It does help to have two teachers as parents."

Avery, a 16-year-old junior at a suburban public high school in the mid-Atlantic, described himself as biracial (White and Asian) and didn't identify as a particularly high-performing or low-performing student. He was also the only student we interviewed who had teachers in his immediate family.

"It does help to have two teachers as parents," he told us. "Now that I'm in tenth grade, they can't help me as much, just . . . because they [teach] lower grades. But overall, they know what I'm going through, what the teacher might be going through—it's just very helpful."

Avery also described how his parents helped him try new strategies when he struggled with knowing how to approach his schoolwork:

> I tried to do some of the articles by myself, but it was really difficult for me. . . . I'm not good with reading online stuff; it's way easier for me to read a book than it is for me to read something on a computer. So, I wasn't doing great on the quizzes. But I asked my dad for some help. And he would reread the question or help me understand it better if I didn't understand it, and help me read through the stuff. And I did much better on it. So, it's definitely easier to have two teachers as parents to kind of guide me through stuff that I don't understand.

What about for the majority of us who aren't teachers? The ways in which Avery described his parents as being helpful are still available to non-teacher parents as well: help them in perspective-taking about what may be going on with the adults in the school building and help them try out new strategies when their existing ones aren't working. Crucially, Avery's parents only offered him this help when he asked for it—and offered it in ways that gave him tools for the future rather than doing it for him. Both of those factors are key (though Avery's story only illustrates them subtly) because, without them, parents run the risk of falling into the trap of overparenting and depriving teens of the agency they need to learn and grow.

Caprielle and Eddie: "My sister was just so aware of it all."

Parents aren't the only family members who can open up possibilities. Any student who is a younger sibling can benefit from the experience and knowledge gained by their older siblings about teachers, electives, extracurriculars, and alternative programs; older siblings are often able to provide even more useful info than parents. Caprielle was completing her final two years entirely through a dual-enrollment program when we spoke with her, a program she'd learned about from her older sister:

> *My sister was just so aware of all of it. . . . She sends me all of the scholarships and resources. And she often found a lot of programs after the deadline or after she was eligible because she's sending me so much more than what she even did. So, I'm a part of so many programs, and I'm even doing a particularly exciting program this summer. I think the big thing is, I don't think I would have had time to apply myself to them if I was in [a traditional] high school. I honestly have so much free time now that I'm doing dual enrollment for these things that I honestly want to prioritize. . . . [Otherwise] I would just have to go through the letdown of not being able to actually apply.*

Of course, Caprielle's example also illustrates how the structure of her dual-enrollment program allowed her the scheduling flexibility to take advantage of all these opportunities; if she had learned about these various programs while still working within the more traditional structure of her early years of high school, she felt like she would have been either disappointed or stressed out and overwhelmed. And if she hadn't learned about them from her sister, she felt certain she would have heard of them too late to effectively apply, even if she'd had the scheduling flexibility her dual-enrollment program created.

Caprielle was not the only student we spoke with who had older siblings who helped pave the way for a more engaging high school experience. Eddie, an 18-year-old high school senior from another suburban area in the Northwest, described himself as Black, a football player, and a budding computer programmer. He didn't see himself as a particularly high- or low-achieving student. Like Caprielle, he also had helpful older siblings. He had participated in interesting elective programs on a technical education campus their public school coordinated with. His siblings' participation in these programs meant his parents were already familiar with them, and that enabled his parents to be more supportive of Eddie's unusual choice to stack all his requirements into his junior year and make his senior year entirely hands-on electives at this alternate campus (which we discuss further in a few pages).

Zimo: "I also really value mentorship."

Zimo, an 18-year-old dual-enrolled senior in his second year of a public on-campus dual-enrollment program in the Southwest, described himself as an immigrant from China (he and his family moved to the U.S. when he was in middle school). Zimo was conscious that neither he nor his parents had much familiarity with American school systems when they moved here from China during his middle school years. However, to Zimo, this was not a significant issue because he found mentors:

> *Should a parent necessarily assume that we always know what we're going to do next? I personally have some idea about what I want to do next, but this is not universal. You cannot assume people know what they want to do. Which is why I also really value mentorship, because mentorship allows people to not know things and helps people understand how they want to find out about these things.*

While Zimo may have been more inclined to notice the need for mentorship because he was very conscious of being in an unfamiliar school system, his description of why it was useful illustrates its value for anyone.

Zimo received mentoring through two different formal programs, and both were helpful. One matched him with a near-peer: someone who was already in college and able to give him guidance about that process. As someone in an online dual-enrolled program already, he knew some things about college coursework but not about college life. The second program connected him with a college counselor, who helped him with a range of college application and financial aid questions and decisions:

> *The first one is called Matriculate. And the other one is called the Matchlighters Scholars Program . . . [In Matriculate] I was matched with a current student in Notre Dame. He turned out to be rather busy starting in the fall, but over the summer, he was pretty helpful to me in terms of just generally being a college student because I wasn't on campus for the '20–'21 academic year and don't have much of an idea as to what to expect for in-person versus online version of the program, and the Matchlighters Scholars, you may notice on the website that these include six hours of work, but that person did way, way*

more than six hours. So, she's most definitely very helpful. She does more than college apps. So [she] helped me a lot with deciding about other things, that sort of thing. So yeah, these mentorship programs do really help me a lot. I would hope that they had some more time to actually help me correct the college list before I realized what was going on. Because, let's be honest, that list just ballooned and ballooned.

As Zimo makes clear at the end, he wished one of these mentors had also helped him realize he was biting off more than he could chew with the number of colleges he applied to. Still, overall, he felt like these mentoring programs were incredibly helpful resources to him, giving him insights and information he otherwise couldn't have accessed. His example illustrates how families who are unfamiliar with high school and college options can supplement their lack of experience by helping students find mentors who can help them see a broader range of choices and understand those choices better. These mentors don't have to be through formal programs—this can happen through informal conversations with older students in the neighborhood, at school, or in religious communities.

Showing Up to Support Students' Choices and Needs

Families can also support their teens in making meaningful choices about how their education unfolds. Deeply engaging with young people around their choices but letting them be the ones to make those choices fuels a crucial element to the kind of sustainable motivation that gives students (and people in general) the energy to continue to learn and grow.

Connor: Show me "I care about your life; I don't want to dictate it."

In addition to his parents' "freedom and flexibility with oversight" approach, Connor's parents empowered his educational choices:

For a lot of my educational career, I've been pretty independent. My parents were never the parents to kind of, like, look over my homework or make sure I was doing the reading. . . . Because the expectation is [that] I need to be doing that on my own. Because one day I will anyway, so why not start early, right? And so, my parents had been very kind of "light touch" on academics; it's been very "I find this opportunity, and I find the way to do it, and I sometimes find the funding for it; I figure it out for myself, and then they give a rubber stamp on it. And we move on." And sometimes I'll have to explain why I'm doing the thing that I'm doing or why I want to go for something. And that takes a little warming up. For example, coming to Western and doing the [living away from home, on-campus dual-enrollment] program that I'm doing right now, it took a little warming up. I first learned about it in middle school. And I kind of had to massage my parents a little bit through doing some guided tours of campus, and of the building that I'm living in, and trying to connect them with administrators and answer their questions and be like, "This is not a scam, I promise." Just working through that was a process, but at the end of the day, they've been supportive of me pushing forward with my academics because that was something that they both weren't able to do. Both my parents didn't graduate college; I'm a first-gen student. And so, I think for them watching me push forward with my own academics and do what I want to do, while they recognize that they can't always be directly helpful with it, they have been supportive of me as a person.

Connor is not just describing his parents encouraging him—he's also describing an environment where he is the one to do the work of discovering and pursuing choices, knowing his parents will ask him questions to help him think it through, not to shut it down.

Of course, as a parent, I was curious about how Connor and his parents built a relationship like that. "We have a genuine interest in each other as independent people," Connor said. For example, their standard dinner table conversation of asking him about his day at school looked a little different than what most families might expect:

You had to find something other than the word "good." And then a tiny thing that you did, and that is the starting point for a conversation. And so I would always engage them on "How was work? What did you do?" And then they would always engage me on "How was school? What did you do?" And just starting with that and coming from a very genuine place. . . . That sort of relationship, and that sort of jumping-off point of just saying, "Alright, my day was fine. Here's why it was fine." Or "My day was okay; here's why I gave a different response that's less positive." Starting with that. And then building off of there, I think, kind of built that emotional bridge between myself, my parents, in saying, we both have our own lives, we both have things that we do, and that's going to be inherently independent of each other. But that's okay. Because I can still ask how your day was. . . . Having that back-and-forth dialogue that can be very casual but still shows that sense of "I care about your life; I don't want to dictate it for you. But know that I want to know what's happening. And I want to know about the events in the world that you're living in. Even if I don't get to see it directly. I just want to know more about you as a person, and what you're about, and what you're doing."

We found this take on the simple end-of-day conversation practice interesting. They didn't do something complex or involved. They didn't go to family workshops on how to raise independent children (or at least, if they did, it wasn't something Connor knew about or mentioned to us). They just treated each other as interesting and independent humans who they loved and were curious about. His parents' questions felt like they were learning about him as an individual. The questions were not invasive because he felt the genuine curiosity, rather than the waiting judgment, behind them. The other noteworthy thing here is Connor's role in this. It wasn't one-sided, with his parents nudging him while he sat, bored and annoyed by their questions, staring at his phone. He was also curious about their days and their lives. He described the mutuality of their relationship as being crucial to his autonomy—not just their treatment of him, in other words, but that he also treated them with respectful curiosity and genuine interest.

Melanie: "Having adults not only [ask], 'What are you interested in?' but sitting down and talking through it."

Melanie often felt like her parents expected her to be someone she wasn't—not only not queer, but also not pursuing a career as a nurse, which they thought was below her capabilities. Melanie wished adults would engage differently with her and her peers about their future career choices:

> I think what would have been a more practical thing that I think would have been very helpful for me and a lot of my peers. We got asked, "What do you want to be when you grow up?" a ton. But there wasn't very much support for us finding that, so I think naturally I gravitated toward healthcare, as many high-achieving students, STEM students who I think—like I know my sister went to college eight years ago ish, most of her

friends went to pre-med because they didn't know what else to do. And that was a good answer for their parents, you know? And most of them aren't doing pre-med anymore. But I think having adults not only [ask], "What are you interested in?" but sitting down and talking through it. Or [asking things] like, "Why would you be interested in that? What does that look like? How can I help you? How can I support you looking more into that? Is that really the right fit?" I think that would have been helpful for me in a non-pressure way. I think my parents tried to do that, and they are still trying to do that, but it's all very much like, "How can we make you not like nursing and like being a doctor more?"

It's not just high-achieving students who want a meaningful understanding of career options that lay before them and help in navigating all those possibilities with genuine interest and care rather than feeling like someone is putting their finger on the scales. Too often, when adults ask, "What do you want to be when you grow up?" it's with a ready (and likely unconscious) judgment about what makes for a good answer to that question or not. As one of our student reviewers put it, "It often feels more like 'what does everyone else want you to be?' rather than 'what do *you* want to be?'"

Elena: "My parents are a lot more open about my education."

Elena, an 18-year-old senior at a public high school in the Southeast, asked that we use either she/her or they/them pronouns in describing them (so you'll see that in the book, we alternate between the two) and described themself as Asian American and "somewhat" of a high-achiever, but only in the areas that were important to them. Elena's parents put less pressure on them to pursue specific academic and career interests than the parents of their friends:

Honestly, I kind of think my household is a little bit different and that my parents are a lot more open about my education. For example, I noticed that [with] a bunch of my friends, their parents didn't really discuss their academic choices with them. So, my parents, after discussing it with them, let me go to a creative magnet art school. Whereas a bunch of other people, like my parents' friends, advised me to go to other, more STEM-related schools because it was seen as more prestigious or academic. . . . [So] I felt like I had more agency over what I was able to do and choose on my path. Obviously, they are not perfect parents; that's like a whole other topic. But I would say academically, I was pretty fortunate because I didn't just follow what they said. They understood that it was me going to high school or me going to middle school, and therefore, they should not be the ones . . . to choose why I did what I did.

Elena especially appreciated this because their parents were swimming against not only the current of other parents in their friend group but against the cultural current of the school district itself.

To Elena, it was clear their school district had no "affinity for creativity. . . . They only reward students who really choose vocational, or even trade, or STEM, careers that are just not [seen as] 'frivolous,' for lack of a better word." Her parents were different:

I guess [my parents] strike me as especially supportive compared to my classmates' [parents] because some of [my classmates] did not really want to get herded onto the IB track because they found other things more fulfilling, but their parents thought it would be better for them—but it was not very good for their mental health.

While, of course, parents prioritize doing what we think is best for our kids, what parent doesn't also wish their teen appreciated them more? We can only imagine how challenging this might have been for Elena's parents—swimming upstream against culture always is—but the payoff, in both their relationship and Elena's motivation, is clear.

Eddie: "Leave my school life alone," but be a safe space to ask for help.

Eddie also appreciated that, generally, his parents were not overly involved. When we asked, "What's the best thing a parent can do to support their kids during high school?" he seemed surprised by the question. "I've never really gone to adults for school help, but even if I did, I don't know what I'd ask them. . . . I always kept quiet about it." Doing this fit with his preference for his parents to "leave my school life alone." In his case, for instance, his mom knew he disliked school, but she wasn't worried about him "because she knew I had a plan." His plan was to take advantage of the opportunity online schooling provided to knock all of his junior and senior level requirements out during his junior year and then make his senior year entirely hands-on electives at the tech-ed campus his school had access to.

But Eddie did have some advice for parents who are concerned about how their kids feel about school:

> *You want to make sure your kids aren't afraid to come tell you if they are doing bad in school because if they're afraid to come tell you about their grades, they're not going to come talk to you about if they hate school, because why would they? It's almost, in a way, if you're already treating grades [like such a big deal], then [hating school] would be even worse because now they don't even want to do any of it, you know? So, first of all, they have to trust you to come talk to you.*

He reflected on how, when he first brought his idea to his parents about stacking all his junior and senior year requirements into his junior year to get them out of the way, they were "at first sort of skeptical, but . . . they trusted me."

When he thought about this trust some more, he saw ways where parents should not just "leave school alone":

I'm not all-knowing or very wise because sometimes you might be going down a pretty bad road. So maybe an option for parents is to be like, "Okay, what would be better than this? What would be the best outcome where you're still getting an education but you're happy?" It's not going to be perfect, but . . . then the student could make a list of things that would help them get into their classes. Not immediately shoot it down . . . make an effort to make sure the plan actually happens.

This kind of respectful partnership, one that is involved but lets students generate their own solutions, is similar to Connor's description of how his parents engaged with him when he proposed going to the Gatton Academy, how Melanie described wishing adults would engage her and her peers about career interests, and how Elena described her parents support compared with the ways her friends were treated. All these teens wanted adults, especially their parents, to treat them and their ideas with warmth, genuine curiosity, and support. Even Eddie, who started by saying that all he wanted was for his parents to leave his "school life alone," felt differently once he stepped back and reflected on times when that might not be the best approach. None of these teens thought they were omniscient or incapable of bad decisions—but, just like any adult would, they wanted to be respected and listened to, even if their ideas seemed strange or risky at first.

What to Do to Build Your Family Sense of Belonging

Parenting, guardianship, or even just being the older sibling of someone going through as much change and development as adolescents is not easy. None of the stories here are intended to add to the culture of parent-shaming, especially mother-shaming, that is already prevalent in American culture. As a parent myself, I regularly remind myself of what a therapist once described to me as the 30/70 rule—I only have to get it right the first time about 30% of the time, and the other 70% of mistakes are opportunities to model to my kids how to repair[17] relationships. That's a reminder I need because, otherwise, I spiral every time I'm short, snappish, or just plain hypocritical with my kids. I aim to be like Connor or Elena's parents, but I know I'll often fall short of my goal.

So, instead of shaming and blaming, what can we do with these stories? Absorb them, mostly. Allow ourselves to inhabit a teen perspective more than an adult one for a little while, even (perhaps especially) when we find ourselves wanting to defend the parenting choices described here. Explore if it's easier to lead with empathy and curiosity, rather than a worry-laden agenda, with the young people we love when we see the overlaps and differences between their lives and the stories shared here. And maybe try out some open and exploratory conversations with those loved ones when we're feeling empathetic and curious.

For example, pick up ideas from Connor's detailed stories on how to approach our kids in conversation: with respectful and genuine interest, the way you would an adult family member or friend you're curious about and haven't heard from in a while. Elena's descriptions of her parents' support for her pursuit of art programs, against the grain of what other parents around them were doing, might also spark ideas. Both of those could even be stories to share with the young people you care about to illustrate how you hope to engage with each other. Sharing Eddie's story could be useful for a young person whose first orientation is to want to be left alone since he started from that position but then ended up reflecting on times when he did think it was appropriate for parents to jump in more. And checking to see whether your questions feel like open curiosity or like pressure, with the differences Melanie described, may also be helpful.

Doing this gets easier for us as parents if we can remind ourselves that it's normal for our kids to display sometimes dramatic changes in their personalities and reactions to us during this time. Right as we have hit our stride parentally and professionally, leaving us inclined toward stability, our kids are going through a major shift. They have to learn from their own experiences, but we want to be able to pass on all the wisdom we've struggled to obtain over our previous decades. The disconnect between these two very different phases of life can often get widened by some of the other normal things that happen to a teen's personality during this key stage of identity development. For example, it's normal for young people to become self-centered during adolescence; it's a natural side effect of trying to figure out their identity, but it can often be disorienting to parents to see a child who previously thought of other people suddenly seem incapable of doing so. It's also normal for a teenager to act like a mature adult in one moment and a young child the next. Development doesn't happen in a straight line; hitting a milestone once doesn't mean they stay there. (If we're honest with ourselves, we can see the same thing in our own personalities, though on a smaller scale: who hasn't had the experience of navigating a really difficult experience well one day and overreacting to something small a few days or weeks later?)

Young people are trying to discern who they are independently from the adults who have historically taken care of them. They need to detach from their families to do so, but they're also still dependent on those same family members for some of their basic needs. This conflict between wanting distance from the adults who take care of them to figure out who they are yet still needing those same adults tends to create a back-and-forth between affection and disdain. This conflict fades over time as young people decide which parts of their families to incorporate into their own sense of identity and which parts to leave on the wayside. But while it's happening, it's hard for both adults and young people alike. Just knowing that may make it easier to respond compassionately to both ourselves and the young people around us.

More Ideas From Experienced Practitioners[18]

Watch out for double standards. Young people value authenticity, and they are keenly aware of hypocrisy. If you espouse a guideline for them that you don't follow yourself, it won't go over well.

Maintain a questioning stance. Using questions to help guide a conversation allows people to come to their own decisions without overtly being told what to do (being told what to do is the best way to get anyone to resist, regardless of age). Almost all the positive examples shared by young people in this chapter featured effective question-asking by the adults around them.

Validate feelings rather than engage in problem-solving. Most of the time, when people are upset or frustrated, they want to feel supported and validated rather than having someone solve the problem for them. If a young person directly asks how to solve the problem, then you can share ideas, but even then, consider if there's a way to build their confidence in solving the problem for themselves.

Create opportunities for one-on-one time. Even the seemingly disinterested teenager does need to talk on occasion. Keep in mind that, for many, talking is best done while there is no direct eye contact or while the body is otherwise engaged. For example, going for drives, going for walks, doing a puzzle, raking leaves, or doing hair all represent times when the pressure of having a conversation feels lifted.

2

Enthusiasm, Care, and Voice

～～～～～

Strong Student-Teacher Relationships

"It's always like, if the teacher's good, if they interact with the students and they're kind, it's really easy to pay attention. . . . When they're not, it's really hard to find their class interesting. . . . There's nothing more helping than a helpful teacher, I guess, [who's] not just teaching the subject just to teach, [who] actually wants . . . to help the students be successful."

\- Avery

"I like how they focus a lot on students. . . . It doesn't matter how many times; they always listen to your questions."

\- Maria

"When you see your teacher as a friend, you're a lot more focused when she's talking to you."

\- Eddie

You don't have to spend much time in pop culture about education to encounter the idea that an amazing teacher can overcome all odds and achieve powerful connection and learning with their students. From well-known older films like *Stand and Deliver* and *Dead Poets Society* to modern work like the recent redo of *Matilda* or the popular comedy TV series *Abbott Elementary*,[19] stories of amazing teachers can be as inspiring as they are unavoidable.

While it's unreasonable to project the need to swim upstream against cultural and structural currents onto individual teachers, we can't ignore the fact that individual teachers play a huge impact on whether or not students enjoy learning. What made it easy or difficult to engage with teachers—their enthusiasm, support, power-sharing, and creativity—held true for interviewees from different regions, economic backgrounds, races, and genders, a pattern upheld in decades of educational research.[20] Students with relationships similar to those described below are more likely to learn, feel safe and confident in their abilities, behave appropriately, and generally succeed in school. The stories in this chapter illustrate what these kinds of experiences actually look and feel like to students and can serve both as inspiration for parents to share with teens wondering what to look for and as ideas for adults in the school building to try.[21]

Enthusiastic Teachers Spark Students' Curiosity

Interviewees often talked about how important it was for their teachers to genuinely be interested in the topics they were teaching. This came up more often in the negative than the positive—almost every student, when asked about their least engaging educational experiences, spoke about times in which they became bored because it was so obvious that their teacher was also bored.

Avery, for instance, described how hard it was to stay focused when "the teacher is just not entertaining; like, their voice is super monotone, [and] they just don't have any . . . charisma. . . . It seems like they don't want to be a teacher. But that's not helpful for students that are told that they need to learn stuff." Likewise, Elena talked about how she had a teacher who "was like a very grumpy worker at the DMV. He was just not into his job at all. And he took it out on the students."

Ariya, a senior at a public high school in the Southeast, laid it out in more detail, alluding to different factors that might contribute to both students and teachers not feeling especially enthusiastic about what's going on in class:

There are just certain teachers who, it's very clear, they don't want to be there. And of course, I always do [think of] teachers' pay and, like, you know, the benefits, and I don't blame them at all; teenagers are frustrating as a whole. But also, kind of, it reflects in how they teach things, and not even the lack of emotion about it, just the lack of innovation with teaching. I have sat in a classroom for hours of my day since I was five. I am sick of it by now. I know, for a fact, a lot of my other peers are also sick of it. So, if you repeat the same structure and foundation of "I'm sitting, and you're lecturing, and then you give me an assignment, and then maybe once a month I have a test," I'm already bored. I'm already checked out. I'm just concerned about passing. I am not at all concerned about actually learning what you're teaching me.

Anyone who has spent time in a classroom can probably relate to what Ariya describes here, but the fortunate have also had experiences with teachers who genuinely loved the subject they were teaching: the English teacher who was still passionate about the books assigned to his students even though he'd heard students discuss that same book for years, the science teacher who loved the experiments they could do in a high school lab, the math teacher who was genuinely enthused about the logical thinking of algebra. Tacitly, when teachers are genuinely interested in their topics, they convey that it's worthwhile to invest time and effort into building abilities and knowledge in that subject.

Eddie: "She was almost more excited about it than we were."

For Eddie, the teacher he most enjoyed working with was one who taught a business elective course he took in his senior year of high school. The way this teacher approached her class with such obvious enthusiasm is what initially got Eddie interested in her class. "She would always tell us about the things she'd done in the past, and the reason she was teaching was definitely because she enjoyed teaching" and not because she lacked other options for making a living. (Her experience in other business ventures also gave her more legitimacy in the students' eyes for teaching their business class).

When it came to the particular business projects the students picked to work on:

> She was almost more excited about it than we were. And that would make us be like, "Oh, she actually cares about what she's teaching, and, you know, this is actually important to her." . . . I feel like a lot of time teachers try to . . . get you to think [the topic is] important without really caring about what they're teaching.

Her passion for the subject piqued his interest, and the fact that she combined it with kindness and engaging, real-world activities preserved it.

Eddie described how when he went "into class, it'd be like talking to a friend"—and how he was particularly impressed because "she played no favorites." He noticed this because he was used to the opposite—Eddie, a football player, had benefited from being treated with obvious warmth and respect from his coaches and noticed how the "benchwarmers" got treated. "You know, the coaches wouldn't be as close with them," whereas with "the cool, athletic kids, they would always be joking around, talking to them in the halls, and stuff like that." Eddie said he usually "didn't blame teachers because some students don't give them . . . the respect they deserve."

But that made it all the more impressive to him when this teacher "[showed] no preference whatsoever, regardless of how . . . weird or strange or different" a student might be and regardless of which of her classes a student was taking.

Instead, "she always paid attention" and remembered what students told her, following up later to ask how things were going and even helping out with extracurricular business-related activities:

> We had a kid who was starting [a business]; he'd mow lawns in the summer and do landscaping. He was like, "Hey, I have no idea how to do finances for this, and taxes," and she's like, "Oh, I know a friend who would help you for free." And she got him acquainted with that friend so he could get help with that.

She also set up her class to have multiple applied opportunities for learning business principles. Her students got involved with local businesses and helped them solve actual business challenges that the businesses were facing.

They also picked a short-term business venture to take on as a class—starting up their own beverage truck business "to take it to school events . . . and just sell drinks there. . . . That was all the way through the whole year until the end, where we finally got it going." Rather than simply being a lesson in the economics of buying materials and selling drinks, the students were involved in every aspect of setting up the business, starting with deciding what venture to take on—they had noticed there were local non-alcoholic drink businesses that were popular, and the teacher "called . . . a drink truck business to come talk to us." After hearing these owners talk about their business, the students liked it. "So that's what we decided on." Then they needed to get the school to agree to buy a used bus, learn how to navigate permitting and inspections, design logos and drink flavors, get the right dimensions for the drink machines, and even "tour a local bag factory in our city, so we could see how the bags were made. So, we can be like, 'hey, when we're designing bags, we should do it with this in mind, so it's easier for us and the bag manufacturers.'" All of this culminated in the students finally being able to sell drinks from the truck they'd put together, with the designs and product choices they'd made, at an end-of-year event. As Eddie put it, "It was really fun. . . . I've never had a class like that; that was so cool."

Throughout the whole experience, the teacher's enthusiasm for what they were doing was really evident to Eddie and his classmates because it was clear she was putting time into making the project work; for example, she was the one often following up on permitting and updating the class each week on the latest status. Her passion was infectious. Of course, her enthusiasm was not the only factor at play here that built Eddie's own excitement for the course—other elements of what she did mirror other themes explored in this and later chapters: she built her students' business skills in a way that felt relevant, she cared for students and even connected them with people in her network that could help them, and she gave them a significant amount of choices to make about how they undertook this business venture together. This example, from a class at a vocational-technical school that was available to students in the more "traditional" public high school Eddie attended, is just one of several shared by interviewees that also illustrates why it's worthwhile for parents and teens to investigate what kind of options may be available in their area that they might otherwise overlook.

Goose: "He would always be so enthusiastic . . . so engaged."

Like Eddie, Goose had an enthusiastic teacher she loved. Unlike Eddie's teacher, however, his enthusiasm didn't require so much extracurricular energy, a distinction that may be helpful for adults looking for ways to connect with students that don't double their workload. "He would always be so enthusiastic about things. I think when you see a person be very passionate about something and just be very kind and, overall, so engaged, I think it makes you want to talk to them more." His enthusiasm for teaching and English was apparent in the way he shared materials with them—for example, he introduced her to the poem "Wild Geese," which she loved so much it inspired the pseudonym she picked for this book. He would also "get so excited" when students made comments about the works they read in class and was interested in their opinions on what they were reading, saying things like "that's so good . . . I didn't think of that."

This enthusiasm for student responses to the topics he was himself interested in carried over in how he gave feedback. Goose noted that when they were working on projects, and someone would call him over to come look at their work thus far, he would "look at it in depth" and say things like, "Wow, this is so good":

> *No matter what you do, he is so willing to be there to look over it and tell you you're doing great. And if you're not doing so great, he redirects you into a good direction. . . . Literally everybody . . . can tell you they felt so smart in his class because he made it really engaging and made everyone feel like they had something really unique to say.*

Goose's example illustrates how important the relationship between enthusiasm for the subject and enthusiasm for how students engage with the subject is to create an engaging classroom experience.

Additionally, because this teacher was so warm and caring to his students, he became a safe person and a mentor for Goose when she was struggling with some mental health challenges in her final year of high school triggered by losing her friend group, a situation described in more detail in the chapter on peers. After falling out with her friends, she began to struggle with anxiety and other intense negative feelings, to the point of wanting to avoid school. So having a teacher whom she had already connected with and felt "very safe talking to" meant that when she was "really first struggling with the whole loss of friends," or even if she was "just having a bad day," she would think, "Oh, at least I have English today. I can see my teacher today."

For Goose, this was "a blessing. . . . He's 67, but he's so open-minded, and so I felt very safe having somebody much older that I could talk to and also just share wisdom with." For her, this made a tremendous difference in her ability to finish out the school year successfully. When we asked whether she'd ever gone to school counselors for support, she said she'd tried but that it seemed to her that their main function was to "actively try" *not* to get students 504s or IEPs,[22] "unless you have something really severe," and to be someplace "people mainly go when they have an emergency. It's not really a place you could go to just talk." In other words, for the more everyday stressors of being a teenager, having a trusted teacher to talk to was the most appropriate and helpful support to Goose, and she was certainly not alone in that impression. Many students we spoke to said they far preferred talking to a trusted teacher over going to school counselors they barely knew. While fostering this kind of trust goes far deeper than mere expressions of enthusiasm, Goose's teacher's enthusiasm for both his subject and how his students engaged with it paved the way for that kind of trust to be built.

Caring Teachers Equip Students to Succeed

Both Eddie and Goose's stories about their enthusiastic teachers reveal more than just passion for their subjects and their teaching of them, of course—woven in with their enthusiasm is also an obvious and genuine care for the students themselves. Almost every interviewee who described an engaging teacher talked at some point about that teacher's kindness, and many students discussed their favorite teachers as being more like older friends they respected. Like Ian, a junior at a public vocational-technical high school in the Northeast, who talked about his "really impressive [economics] teacher." To Ian, it was clear:

> *Every single student, we were his friend. And when he gave lessons and things, he would make sure every single student understood what it was; like when we got an assignment, . . . you could check with him no matter when or what he was doing. If you said you needed help, he would immediately stop what he was doing, and he would help you.*

This theme of caring about students and being happy and able to help them learn whenever they needed help often made the key difference between the teachers students felt they learned a lot from and those they didn't.

Avery: "If you need help, he'll come right over and just focus all his attention on you."

For instance, Avery contrasted one of his least favorite teachers with one of his most favorite by describing how the "good" chemistry teacher would always make sure students actually understood when they asked questions, whereas a particularly unhelpful math teacher he had would just repeat his same confusing explanations over and over. "Fairly recently, I didn't understand something, and I asked him. He explained it the exact same way. I asked him again, and he explained it in the same way and thought that I understood it. I felt forced to say yes, right? Because he explained it to me two times." Maria had a similar experience with one of her math teachers, who just taught "one way," so she "needed to teach [herself] the work." To her, this felt like the teacher was "not focusing on the students in this school" because she wasn't responding to what they needed to learn.

Additionally, Avery said that the helpful chemistry teacher he was contrasting with his unhelpful math teacher doesn't "try to get to know you, but if you need help, he'll focus all his attention onto you." When asked what this looked like, Avery described how "he'll teach . . . and then he'll hand us a worksheet or a lab, which is either partner work or single work. And if you raise your hand, if you need help, he'll come right over and just focus all his attention on you for however long you need it until you understand."

Grace: "He cared about us, not just the student version of us."

Grace will always remember and appreciate her IB World History teacher, whom she took classes with in her junior and senior years of high school:

He made it a point to not only teach us world history (which really meant the history of Europe and some parts of Asia) but also to keep us socially and politically updated on current world news. Every Friday served as a "make-up" day, where we could finish his work from the past week and finish work for other classes. As he put it, "You are all becoming young adults who are learning time management, so I cannot stop you from work-ing on assignments for other classes if you've finished this class's work." On make-up days, in the background, he'd put on a video from The Daily Show with Trevor Noah.[23] He would contextu-alize the news and condense it in a way that we could better understand it. In his words, "Since y'all are about to be func-tioning citizens in society, you should know what's going on in the world." I really appreciated knowing that a teacher, a White teacher who was teaching predominantly students of color, cared enough to do his job as a history teacher in addition to making us educated young adults. Thinking back on it, I wonder how he was able to fit these Friday sessions into his course plan-ning, but either way, it was evident that he cared about us. It's not like he cared only about the student version of us but also about the version of us that was about to make decisions based on what we saw on TV and on social media.

His approach made it clear to Grace that "he was a student advocate. Not only were these Fridays a nice break from the usual IB curriculum, but I felt like I was being filled in on the social and political gaps of my formal school education."

And from what Grace remembers, all of the students loved it. "His lighthearted humor, good-natured and down-to-earth personality, and his ability to teach us about headline news made us respect him more. . . . Both Trevor Noah and my high school teacher treated the news with a mixture of humor and solemnity that made us respect them more."

In fact, Grace enjoyed and trusted his teaching so much that he became her African American History teacher my senior year.

Despite the potential for it to be awkward to have a White man teaching this course, I never thought the way he handled his identity in relation to the course content was inappropriate. It was during the spring semester of my senior year—a year after

George Floyd's murder and a year after the Black Lives Matter movement gained greater national attention—and it was during a time in which people were gravitating toward understanding African American history and the history of injustice in our country. I can only imagine the pressure he might've felt. But I thought he was the best man for the job in the context of my school. At the time, my high school was predominantly Black and Latino [sic] (roughly 88% of the student population), while the majority of the faculty were White. In high school, I was comfortable with this image because it seemed to me that my teachers were equally aware of the power dynamic and privilege they held as a result. I'm sure there was some part of me that probably should've thought that it was a little strange that a White man was about to teach me about African American history, but I didn't think it was strange at all. In fact, it was the previous respect I had for him as my World History teacher and student advocate that made me trust him.

As the year went by with the course, Grace recalled several instances where he would acknowledge his Whiteness in the context of the course. To her, his acknowledgment of this power dynamic eased the subtle tension in the classroom.

Grace also felt he was able to take a lot of productive liberties with this course because it was an elective:

He structured the course to spend less time on the older history of injustice to Black Americans, such as slavery and the Civil War era, and more time on the continued injustice of the 20th century. He emphasized more on the parts of African American history that he knew weren't being taught in detail in our other history courses, which included, but were not limited to, the time periods after the Civil War, race riots and massacres, the treatment of Black veterans, the similarities of ideology between Martin Luther King Jr. and Malcolm X, the history of voter suppression, all of which seemed to have paralleling themes of the news during that time of early 2021.

For Grace and her peers, "all of this conveyed to us that he was invested in supporting our learning and success more so than checking boxes or playing it safe, which caused us to trust him even more and for the class to feel relevant and engaging."

Melanie: "I think when teachers care about you, you want to do well in their class."

Melanie talked about three teachers whom she had found especially engaging—her Spanish teacher, her English and civics teacher, and her chemistry teacher. When asked what made these teachers stand out, she said, "I think when teachers care about you, you want to do well in their class, you want to please them, you want to . . . give them what they're giving you in that way. So yeah, I think that's been my experience with these three teachers; they've all just cared so deeply about their students." Her description of deep caring matches how Eddie, Goose, and other students described their relationships with their most engaging teachers.

Melanie had a couple of teachers who really pushed her academically but provided a lot of support to reach those high expectations. Her chemistry and pharmaceuticals teacher was one of these:

So, during honors chemistry, it was tough. . . . I think it was the first course I'd ever taken that I actually felt very challenged. So yeah, she would check in with us, like for attendance. She'd do a fun question that we all answered. When we did [badly] on tests, she would have a chat with us, like "I'm not mad at you; I'm disappointed," but it was very much like she cared about us, how we were learning. She was always available for extra help . . . after periods. She was pretty responsive over email. And she just genuinely wanted to hear what was going on in our lives outside of chemistry.

This same chemistry teacher also helped students during the COVID lockdown, which started in Melanie's sophomore year, by having "office hours to get help. Most teachers did recorded lectures, and she did too. But she, on Friday mornings, a couple of my friends and I would hop on and just talk. . . . Having that outlet just to talk. . . . for an hour every Friday morning was really nice."

She had a somewhat similar experience with an AP Calculus BC class, one that was even more challenging at the start:

I remember at the beginning of the year, me and my best friend, we would be on the verge of tears every class, like, "What is going on? We're in the wrong class. I have no idea what she's talking about." But I think she made it very clear from the first day; "this will be a hard class. You're gonna have several hours of homework every night. It's gonna be intensive." But we also, I think we trusted her because we'd heard testimonials of her teaching. Like her. . . average test score on the AP exam was 4.8. So, like, very excellent. . . . Also, when we went to her after those first tests that we failed [and said], "Oh, I'm so stressed. I don't understand," she [said], "Just come and get help. I am here after school. Some days, I'm here till seven. I can help you; we can work through it. You'll be okay if you do the work." And it was very reassuring, I think, to have that.

When we asked if Melanie trusted this teacher not only academically but also personally, she said, "Yeah, she's a nice lady. I trusted what she said [that] we would be okay. And . . . I definitely chatted with her a couple times about [how] I'm big into birding and hiking. She gave me places to go. It was definitely nice." In other words, Melanie wasn't as close with this teacher as she was with some of the others she talked with us about, but she did believe the teacher was kind and interested in her success and overall well-being.

Melanie had other teachers who invested in her both academically and personally, most notably an English teacher who also taught a civics elective (she took both) and a Spanish teacher with whom she took multiple classes. Her English/civics teacher "was an interesting guy. He's very opinionated. He's very bold, very interesting." She described his class as "extremely engaging because we had these discussions about current events and how we were doing." He sparked other conversations too:

> *I remember at the end of the first quarter, we just had a day where we went around in a circle and just answered fun questions like, "If heaven is real, what do you want God to say to you when you get there?" Or like, "If you went to jail, what crime would it be for?" Fun questions that just kind of brought us together. It was definitely a very bonded community. And he did a really good job of, like, half the kids were at home, half the kids were in school, of creating that community where people can talk.*

Being able to successfully create a sense of community even in a hybrid environment—something anyone who has joined in on a meeting where some of the people are in person and some are on a screen can relate to the challenge of—was not this teacher's only accomplishment. But it was a vital foundation for his approach to not only his English and civil conversations classes but even the "civil conversation" club he sponsored. "He's very big into civil dialogue, and just talking through issues, and learning from each other in that way."

This emphasis on thinking critically in conversation with each other paved the way for him to shift student mindsets about focusing so heavily on grades:

His [other] big thing was, "I want you to learn; it's not about a grade." So especially for AP Language [with] him, especially with an AP class, it's difficult to let go of those grades. And he was pretty good about that; like his grading of essays was holistic, it wasn't often a rubric. He gave us participation grades [where] we could pick the grade and then you gave a justification. So, I think he was very good at that.

It also helped that, despite being very opinionated and bold, "he was also quite approachable." Melanie described how "he was very responsive" when she went to him about "some personal issues." She explained, "It just made me feel very seen to have an adult, for the first time, that cared, and I felt safe opening up to."

Melanie later also formed a close relationship with a Spanish teacher, who became her "favorite teacher" despite the fact that initially, at the start of junior year, "I didn't like her very much. . . . I thought she was fake. . . . She yelled at me once for getting up too early at the end of [the first] class. So, I [thought], 'She's annoying; she's mean.' But no, she's the nicest person I've ever met." At the time of our interview, which was at the end of her senior year, Melanie described how now "I chat with her regularly about life or whatever. And Spanish is never something—I always thought it was kind of boring, but [now] it's my favorite class because . . . she's just very kind, very genuine."

Being able to fully return to school her senior year and "be able to talk to [her] teachers again" was especially important for Melanie. She had stronger reasons than some students to find connections in school; her mom had been undergoing cancer treatment for years, and at one point, Melanie needed to live with her older sister while her parents stayed in a bigger city for extended treatments:

Having good relationships with teachers has also been really big for me. I think that a little bit [goes] back to my mom being sick.

That was from, like, eighth grade through eleventh grade. So, during a lot of that time, they had their own issues. They had a lot going on, my parents, during my summer before my sophomore year. I spent a couple of months with them in New York City, for treatment during the summer. Then, throughout that year and during COVID, there was treatment going on. And I think school was very much like an escape.

Melanie recalled one particular moment when she went to her Spanish teacher for help. She was concerned about how anxious she was feeling and how she was having trouble sleeping. She recalled the following exchange with her teacher:

Melanie: Hey, can we chat for a couple minutes?

Teacher: Yeah, sure, have a seat. What's up?

Melanie: I've been so on edge and anxious. I feel like I'm going crazy. I don't know, is this normal? What is going on?

Teacher: Yeah. You're not alone; it is normal. You've got a lot going on. It's very heavy, but it's normal; you don't have to feel like you're going crazy.

For Melanie, this exchange "brought me back to earth a little bit because I was already thinking of . . . all the possible disorders I could have. . . . But at the same time, [she] validated what was going on. So that was just really helpful; even the 15 minutes she took just to sit down and talk just made me feel so much better." What meant even more was that the next day, her teacher shared an app with her, saying, "Here's this app I use sometimes; it helped me fall asleep; maybe it'll help you too." For Melanie, that "just meant the world to me, even just those very small gestures." Overall, Melanie felt that her relationships with her Spanish, English, and chemistry teachers helped her not only stay engaged academically but also weather very stormy periods in her home life.

Layla: "She was so strong on . . . making sure you learned the material."

Like Melanie, Layla also formed an especially close relationship with one of her teachers:

> *My most engaging learning experience had to be my junior year of high school chemistry class. My teacher was from Egypt, and it was her first year teaching chemistry after getting her master's. Being from Egypt as well, [along with] another student, it felt so familiar to be able to speak my home tongue with the both of them. She also was so strong on the point of making sure you learned the material—not just passing; like how if you needed extra time to understand homework, she would give you extensions to get her help and leave empty grades instead of putting zeroes for missed work, so you can still hand it in without being afraid of asking for help. . . . The fact that there was no deadline, I used to joke like, "I can't even hold myself accountable; I need somebody to make a deadline," but realistically, I guess the social aspect of "she gave me leeway to do it, to take as much time [as I needed], so I need to give it to her as soon as possible" was more respect-based, like trust- instead of fear-based, and I felt like since she was genuinely looking to help me, I can't do her wrong, and it motivated me to want to do my work.*

This teacher's approach to prioritizing mastery of content over grade and time-oriented performance may have been informed by educational research in this area, especially given that she was recently out of graduate school. Mastery-based learning[24] is one of the most-studied instructional techniques, with several decades of research behind it, and focuses on having each student demonstrate a basic level of competency with a skill before moving on to the next skill or concept.

Regardless of whether this educational research informed her chemistry teacher or not, the obvious investment in her learning and success had a significant impact on Layla—as she succinctly put it, "It actually made me love chemistry."

Beyond the benefits of the mastery approach, Layla's chemistry teacher also helped Layla in another way:

She made me understand that if there's one thing I'm bad at and there's one thing I'm good at, just keep practicing that thing I'm good at, and then, worst comes to worst, when I try that bad thing again, I still have a good thing instead of [becoming] bad at both, [and then having it turn into] "that's it. End game." And I just miss it. Honestly, I want to visit her one day; I miss her so much. She doesn't understand her impact, like me realizing how I needed to learn and my learning style for later on in life.

This self-knowledge turned out to be especially vital for navigating challenges in her university classes in subsequent years.

For example, in her first year of college, Layla discovered her science professors and peers looked down on students who asked questions to seek to understand the content. In contrast, with her high school chemistry teacher:

I never felt intimidated, even with so many questions that were just literally outright stupid. [For example, I asked] if hydrogen could be split, and she was just like, "I literally answered this," . . . but she was just so joking and fun that it [made] learning an experience rather than [just] a thing you have to do to learn the next thing, to learn the next thing, [and so on]. If that's the case of learning, then what's the point? Because I know it won't be applied that way. Everything I've learned interest-based has somehow been added to my life. But everything I've learned forcefully has not been put in the way that I learned it.

We discuss the harmful effects of being in an educational environment that prizes the performance of knowledge over actual learning in the peers chapter, but here, it's worth noticing the role Layla's *relationship* with her teacher plays. With a friendly teacher who invested in students' learning, Layla (and other students in the class) not only learned difficult material but also grew to enjoy a subject they previously hadn't been interested in.

Nina: "They would get involved to support us to go bigger and to be more successful."

In contrast to Layla and Grace's experiences, Nina was the only full-time college student[25] we spoke with who had found particularly strong connections with and support from her first- and second-year college faculty. Nina, a 22-year-old sophomore at an open-access state college in the Southeast, had completed her high school diploma via homeschooling by the age of 17. She described herself as a White woman who had moved around several times as a kid and teenager and who hadn't felt especially connected to any of the communities she lived in as a result. One notable and thought-provoking difference between Nina's college experience and that of Layla and Grace's was that, where both of them were at "competitive" universities, Nina was at an open-access college. She had deliberately made the decision to save money on her first two years of college by getting an associate's degree that would transfer to a more prestigious four-year institution.

Nina was also unlike our other interviewees in that she was one of only two (King being the other) who had been homeschooled for high school. Whereas this was an incredibly positive experience for King, for Nina, it generally wasn't. (Although she may not have appreciated the independence it gave her since, unlike King, she didn't have the experience of public school for comparison.) After completing her high school equivalent at 17, she decided to wait to start college until she knew what she wanted to do with her degree. So, she worked for two years before enrolling in her local state college to pursue an associate's degree. Initially, she felt a little lost and didn't have anyone she felt she could turn to because neither of her parents had finished college, and she had no older siblings with college experience either:

> *I felt very like, "I don't even know what to do. I don't know any of the processes. I don't know anything." And I was actually just talking [today] with one of my professors—he's one of the greatest mentors I've had—about my first semester and how I wasn't connected with anything.... If only I knew all of the things that I could be connected with because I feel like that semester was just a waste. Like I could have done so much more.*

This mentor was one of the professors she worked with in the interdisciplinary honors program at her college. She credited their approach to those classes and the community they built—student to professor and student to student—with changing her entire college experience.

It was particularly impressive to Nina how the professors in the unique group-teaching model honors program managed to do that even when there were COVID distancing restrictions in effect:

> *You can't not have a "community" sense with them. It's impossible—just because there's physical distance, you know, they're so excellent at creating a sense of . . . emotional and academic, intellectual connection. . . . I didn't feel like I was lacking even if there were some times where physically we have to stay six feet apart, but it was still "[we're] figuring out this problem together." It was still that sense of togetherness. . . . They would*

get involved to support us to go bigger and to be more success-ful. . . . It was the equal distribution of eagerness and excitement and, you know, investing. Like they really invest their time in what we're doing and what we care about so that we can be the most successful at it, which is not something I'd experienced before.

Nina's description revealed another way that educators can invest in student success and well-being—by creating structures that build a community out of the classroom. This was possible for the program because it was a more interdisciplinary, project-based curriculum—a model that more high schools and middle schools have begun to adopt in recent years, even though none of our interviewees had experienced it in secondary school. Nina also reiterated a theme that showed up again and again in interviews, including those that have already been discussed above—that educators who "invest their time in what we're doing, and what we care about" are very engaging to students.

However, what this "investment" looked like from the two professors who were leading the honors program at the time she was taking it was different. One of the professors, the one she described as one of her greatest mentors, really pushed her from the very first day she started. She came in feeling a bit shy because she joined the program a semester later than most of the students, having found out about it from another student in her math class in her first semester of college. She sat in the back of the classroom on the first day:

Because all of the people in the class had already connected with one another in the first semester, I even felt more like an outsider. It was like, "Okay, I'm gonna have to get in the cliques. I'm gonna have to find my people." . . . So [the first professor] comes rolling in . . . and probably within the first 20 minutes, he points me out, and he's like, "What's your name?" And I was like,

"Nina." . . . And throughout the whole class, all the questions he was asking, he's like, "Nina, what is it? What is this?" And he was picking on me, and he was, you know, I think trying to bring me out of my shell a little bit, and so he was being [himself]. And I appreciated that because this is how I like to interact with the world. I like to be, you know, "tell it to me straight," so I immediately was like, "Okay, at least this one, I can trust this one."

As she described this story, Nina was chuckling throughout, smiling at the memory of her initial arrival—trying to be quiet and get the lay of the land, while her professor clearly had other plans for how she was going to acclimate into their community. Though, for some, this interaction might sound intimidating, for Nina, it was perfect. It was counterbalanced by the second professor, who came in the latter half of the class. The second professor was far more soft-spoken, but both were equally focused on building community with and *between* the students and rapidly integrating Nina into the community that had already been built the previous semester.

For Nina, getting into this program and this community in her second semester gave her the exact push she needed to really feel like she was fully creating her own unique college experience and connecting with the faculty and peers in it. Prior to that, she'd felt adrift:

I would be a part of class, and then I would maybe go in, buy something from the cafeteria. I would walk around for maybe 20 minutes, and then I would just be like, "Okay, I'm done." No sense of the "college experience" because I just didn't know where to turn. . . . I didn't even necessarily want to be around because . . . it was too scary for me at the time to take that stance and just talk to random people.

For Nina, "the contrast of the community versus lack thereof" was stark. In this program, she'd felt she had "no choice but to be connected." She added:

You have no choice but to participate. You would stick out if you didn't speak up in class. Basically, that was just the environment that they created. And I think that's really where I thrived because it pushed me to my limit, and then I realized that "Oh, no, I like this. I'm comfortable being pushed." Pretty much all the connections that I've made ended up coming from [this program].

It wasn't until she came into a program where the faculty were focused both on their individual relationships with students and on building community between students that Nina's experience shifted for the better. She went from struggling to make connections to feeling like she was part of a community, and that gave her the motivation to seek out even more opportunities in subsequent semesters.

Strong Relationships Also Enable Student Voices

Connor: "She made it really meaningful by really starting with relationships."

In seventh grade, Connor had an encounter with a teacher that deeply impacted him even to this day:

My school at the time was trying to be like, 'Hey, really engage with your students, really try to ask them how you could be doing things differently.' But very few teachers actually did it, and when they did, they often got these pro forma responses.... It didn't feel very meaningful." But with one particular science teacher, it was different. Students believed that she would actually listen to what they had to say. "She made it really meaningful by really starting with relationships, really starting with empathy first, and then . . . breaking down and building out those ideas of what can we be doing better, how can I be improving as a teacher, how can I make this content more engaging?

Connor explained that she built those relationships by making time to have one-on-one conversations with students at least once a month, either during a more open "home period" his school had at the end of the school day or during class while students were doing independent work. In these conversations, she'd seek out their feedback or sometimes "talk about what the student was feeling, what their life was about, trying to build out that personal connection." That way, "when that conversation about 'how could we be doing this better?' came up, the student was more likely to engage deeply and provide more valuable information." For Connor, this was both surprising and refreshing. "I've never seen another teacher do that sort of thing, that sort of empathy and that sort of interest in the students, in general."

Connor also said her interest in really using their feedback showed up in how she used her time. "She would sometimes even use her planning periods to have these longer conversations. I remember she specifically carved out a planning period to kind of workshop [class ideas]." She would share what she was thinking and hearing and then say, "I just want to hear from a student; what are you thinking about?" Her obvious investment mattered and left a lasting impression on Connor. "Being 13 years old and sitting in my science classroom, and watching a teacher do that, that was incredible; that was something that was really exceptional."

She further built their trust by altering her assignments based on their interests. For instance, when they got to a unit about tectonics and earth science—or, as Connor jokingly put it, the "here's all the natural disasters you need to be worried about unit"—she made it more interesting by "concocting a project based on the input from various students. . . . There were some that wanted to be artists, some that wanted to be architects, and some that were really interested in engineering and modeling." She invited them to use those interests to either collaborate with each other in groups or work independently to create models that illustrated potential responses to different natural disasters:

> *Like a building that could survive a volcano or a tsunami, or a really detailed evacuation plan, or different things like that, so that we could have more interesting ideas ... on what's happening, and better understand what's already being done around that. ... So, you learn about the thing, but you extrapolate it out to what's the project, what's something I can play with here, get my hands dirty.*

The ability to play around and make choices that combined their interests with what they were learning made the assignment more engaging and showed Connor and his classmates that their teacher was really listening to their feedback. "Everyone kinda loved it," which, for previously disengaged students, was quite a change.

When asked whether the teacher explicitly laid out how she was using their feedback to inform the project, Connor said that wasn't how she approached it:

> *I know that she asked me about it; I know that she asked other students about it, but really, what it came down to [was] building on the interest that a lot of students were expressing, the idea of "I want students to engage in this, and students are saying that me lecturing at the front of the class doesn't really help them engage." She was experimenting with these different formats, and she found that doing these kinds of presentations helped with that. ... It wasn't that she got in front of the class and said, "I'm doing this based on your feedback." It was that she said, "We're doing this now," which implicitly was informed by the kind of feedback she had been getting throughout the year.*

Later, Connor pointed out that he didn't want to sound like he thought it was the perfect ideal—his subsequent work with the Kentucky Student Voice Team[26] taught him how valuable it was for teachers to "tell students how their feedback is being used . . . so there's more of a two-way street between the student and teacher."

Despite the lack of an explicit two-way street, this teacher's investment in student input caused Connor to start thinking of education differently:

> It kind of opened my eyes to the fact that I should have a say in my education. . . . Because, at the end of the day, if [the problems I see] aren't solved during the time I'm in school, it's going to affect me, and there's no telling how it's going to be affecting other people later on down the line. And so that made me realize I should be involved in these conversations. And then, over time, [as I noticed] more and more problems within my school system and education policy in general, [I realized] there needs to be some sort of change, especially as the world evolves and adapts.

So, he started to get involved with his school system locally by becoming a student advisor to the school board, an experience we discuss more in a later chapter on student autonomy. Connor was deeply appreciative that this teacher sparked a new approach to his education and the role he could play in it in the ways she connected with students and sought out their opinions on how learning could unfold in her classroom.

Nina: "You trusted me with this, and now I'm going to take care of it."

Nina's favorite professors were similar to Connor's science teacher. When asked about what made the biggest difference in her engagement, she said, "What really propelled me was being taken seriously and given a voice." She spoke about how even the fact that her honors program professors advocated for being addressed by their first names surprised her at first. But then:

> *I appreciated it because it's like . . . "I'm an adult, you're an adult." And I had an insecurity when I first started, for starting later. . . . I'm not straight out of high school . . . I don't live with my parents. I have a job; I'm not just a student. And so, I was nervous to see who I could connect with. I think that made me appreciate that level of respect even more.*

Because of how connected and empowered she felt in the community-oriented honors courses, she started to seek out other opportunities to get more involved on campus:

> *I happened upon the . . . Cultural Diversity Committee, and I realized . . . there were no students on the committee. . . . I thought that was interesting. . . . It seems like if it's a committee for college students, I'd be interested to hear what students have to say. I got connected with them, and I became the first student on the committee, which was really cool. And so, it was those kinds of things; I wanted to leave my time in [college] feeling like I did something, [even if it was] just impacting one person. But the way that I happened upon it was different than I expected. It really made me value every kind of networking connection, so when opportunities like that come about, I'm like, "Yes, absolutely." Because it's so, so valuable to me to do anything to step out and just meet another person [who] values learning, values people.*

The other "kinds of things" she's referring to were the Writing Center, the Democratic Club, and the honors program.

In particular, she was given an opportunity at the intersection of her work as a peer tutor in the Writing Center and as a student from the honors program that was really meaningful to her. She was invited to become a "writing fellow" embedded in the classroom of the honors courses, where she went into the classes she'd already taken to be a tutor and provide peer support to students:

> *I think that experience, in particular, has been the most amazing for me because I was chosen [by the honors professors and the head of the writing center]. . . . So, I think that connection and experience was the most beneficial because I was brought in and now . . . I'm able to share my experiences. They've given me the freedom to lesson plan in a sense . . . I have 30 minutes to talk to the other students, and . . . whenever I am given something that I can make my own, and it's trusted with me, that's like being known. I feel so motivated to just propel forward and make it the best that I can because I'm like, "You trusted me with this, and now I'm going to take care of it, and I'm going to make it even better, and let it flourish."*

The fact that she experienced significant benefits from serving in this kind of role is not unique to her. In fact, there was a study[27] of over 120 writing center tutoring alumni from three different institutions that showed that those who had served as peer tutors developed, among other things, "skills, values, and abilities vital in their professions, . . . families, and in relationships, [and] earned confidence in themselves." In Nina's case in particular, the "earned confidence" connects directly to the trust and responsibility she was entrusted to help create the environment for the newer honors program students, allowing her to not only have an amazing and beneficial experience for herself, but also to contribute actively to the community building and support for newer students that had made such a difference for her in her first year of college. All of this was enabled by the educators and administrators who encouraged her to exercise her voice.

What to Do to Support Strong Teacher-Student Relationships

When I heard the stories of all these amazing educators, I couldn't help but be awed and inspired by them. Amidst incredibly challenging circumstances (several of the above stories were set during COVID, and being a teacher was hard even before that), these teachers helped their students not only learn academic content but grow personally. As an educator myself, I can't help but add an extra caveat to anyone reading this who is tempted to judge the teachers they know, themselves or others, and count them lacking. There are *so many* factors that influence a teacher's success, from state or district mandates to interpersonal dynamics with colleagues and students. It doesn't help that teachers are judged by how well students do on standardized tests, not by how curious, engaged, or connected their students are.

Even for those teachers who are invested, who do many of the things described here, they can still have students who are disengaged and disinterested in their class. One example: Zimo noted that he had one instructor who is "a very passionate teacher," who "everyone [else] worships" and who he likes as a person, but the difficulty of reading the teacher's handwritten notes in class, combined with Zimo's disinterest in the class content, meant that he just couldn't engage deeply.

No educator is going to be able to hit 100% student engagement—even in the idealized movie renditions of amazing educators, there's always that one student holding out, and in real life, that number is generally higher, even for teachers at the top of their game.

It's also unreasonable to expect every educator to be at the top of their game. They're as human as anyone else and regularly asked to serve as the human fix for structural weaknesses—like the parable of the child sticking his thumb in the leak in the dam, an individual throwing themselves into the cracks can only hold for so long. The teachers who are willing to do this should be celebrated and acknowledged, yes, but they also should be supported so they don't break under the strain of occupying that role. Most teachers come to education with excitement and joy in the development of young minds and a passion, excitement, and creativity for their subject matter. Yet what confronts them day to day are overly large classes, lack of time, lack of support, lack of resources, being measured on scores rather than on relationships or student development, and an unrelenting stream of young people who have a wide variation of needs and interests in a setting that expects the teacher to mash all that variety into identical outcomes.

It is especially ironic that in an American culture that prizes individualism (especially individuals who forge their own path to obtain success), we have an educational system that generally expects children to match a single standard and simply follow directions without any meaningful autonomy. These amazing teachers worked against this pressure to treat students as humans deserving of care and support.

So, for parents who are looking to support young people in school, it's worth thinking about how to support the amazing teachers who go above and beyond to connect with and promote student learning. Talk with your kids about which teachers they appreciate, and then encourage them to tell their teachers why they're making a difference and ask them what students and families can do to support them. Not only will this make it more likely these teachers stick around—remember, their motivation requires a sense of ability, belonging, and choice, too—it may help your teen feel that sense of belonging more deeply and see how they have the ability to make a positive difference in someone else's life. For those parents and other adults who have the time and energy, it's also worth getting involved in education at the district or even state level and encouraging teens to do the same, to advocate for changes that would make it easier for teachers to connect with, support, and empower their students.

And if you're an educator who is searching for ideas, focus on how many of the most powerful experiences interviewees shared came from just feeling like their teacher genuinely cared about them. Starting there can allow you to build the kind of trust with students that can make it possible to delegate to students the opportunity to make class more engaging by asking them what would make the difference and sharing the responsibility with them for creating that change. This both reduces the burden on you, shifts experiences from being patronizing toward being meaningful, and allows young people the autonomy they need at this stage in their lives to develop and thrive.

To sum it up, here's the advice Connor said he'd give to adults, educators or parents, who are looking to find one thing they can do to help the young people they know:

Oftentimes, parents feel disconnected from their kids, and a lot of teachers feel similarly, but just working with [students] first and coming from a place of not wanting to lecture and immediately make change, but a place to really hear them out and understand . . . is your step zero to fixing a lot of the problems you see in education. . . . Talk to them, ask what they're thinking about and worried about, what they're spending their time doing and why, and if they do care. Because oftentimes, when students say they don't care, they actually do care a lot; it's just not about the thing they think you're asking about. . . . At the end of the day, it's hard not to care about something we're spending 40 hours a week or more doing. . . . Hearing students out and letting them use their voice and right to respect themselves is one of the most powerful things you can do.

We certainly can't say it any better than that.

More Ideas From Experienced Practitioners

For Families:

- Model what it looks like to appreciate and support good teachers. Write a message to the teacher your student speaks positively of, letting them know what you appreciate about them. Ask them what support they need from parents, and work with your teen and other parents to provide it.

- Please don't send messages to your kids during school hours, and reinforce the importance of having phones fully locked away during class time. No teacher can compete with devices built to snare attention.

- Support your child in advocating for themselves rather than leading the charge for them. Help them brainstorm and connect them to others who can help, but let them have the experience of exerting their agency and pushing for change. For instance, rather than finding out who the best teachers are yourself, give them the idea of chatting with older students to find out the best teachers to seek out.

For Educators:

- Get to know your students individually. Assign a portion of class time in the first month of the year to do one-on-ones with students. You'll make up for the "delay" in content later when your students learn more because they trust and relate to you and because you're better able to help them see the connection between the content and their interests. Relationships are essential to motivation, and you'll benefit from their motivation.

- Remember that teens have a highly attuned bullshit detector. Even slight double standards or inauthenticity will get noticed, and any adult who displays them will be dismissed. Don't pretend to be into something your students like to try to win their approval; be genuine and authentic about your interests and passions, and you'll create space for them to share their own.

• Maintain unrelenting positive regard for all your students. This is both the most difficult thing to do and the most singularly useful thing to do. Because of that highly attuned bullshit detector, young people know if you don't like them, even if you're unflaggingly polite and neutral in your comments and behavior. Push yourself to see struggling students as someone trying to learn rather than someone who gives up too easily, and to see seemingly apathetic students as people using a very effective defense mechanism for not having agency. If you can find something to genuinely like about each of your students as humans, even if they aren't "good students," you'll find it easier to maintain your own motivation over time. This will do more for you, and for them, than stressing yourself out trying to come up with exciting activities and new pedagogical techniques.

3

From Distractions to Study Buddies

Peers Influence Learning

"I tell them [other students] to focus on the people that make them happy. And surround yourself with good energy because it's so easy to get caught up in bad energy that's around you ... And I've learned that that makes the worst time, surrounding yourself with bad people, either 'bad' as in they do bad things, or bad people who are jealous of you or not rooting for you."

- Ava

"I think what was honestly really important to make my classes engaging was to have peers in them that I was friends with, that I was willing to talk to. . . . I've been very lucky all four years of high school to have friends in my classes and kind of like my best friends in almost all my classes."

- Melanie

Adolescence is, from a neuroscientific perspective, an incredibly fascinating time period. The brain is learning and changing incredibly rapidly (comparable only to the first year or so of life), and two things, in particular, are going on that make this time period both exciting and sometimes fraught: social approval from peers begins to matter a lot more than adult opinions, and young people are trying to figure out who they are, and want to be, as distinct individuals. Peer relationships begin to matter a lot more, in other words, and influence how young people feel far more than their relationships with adults. It's inevitable, then, that peers will also play a role in how motivated young people feel about their learning environment. The stories shared below illustrate just some of the ways, negative and positive, that students affect each other in school and how our interviewees navigated those experiences. And while adults have far less influence over how these peer relationships unfold than they do over their own relationships with young people, it's still important to understand the ways peers can hinder or help learning in order to get the full picture of the role relationships play in student motivation.

Sometimes, Students Need a New Environment

For some students, negative experiences with peers prompted them to find other learning environments in which to learn. Though this isn't always possible, the stories on how and why students did this might spark useful ideas for students struggling in school because of their peers.

Caprielle: "No part of me regrets leaving [my school]."

Caprielle ended up completing her final two years of high school online through a dual-enrollment program that was publicly available at her local community college. She made this decision in part because she didn't particularly like the social dynamics at her private high school. Caprielle noticed there was a general "cliqueiness" about her school's social dynamics, like there are in most high schools, and she disliked the contrast between that and the smaller and more inclusive private middle school she had come from. As one illustration of the dynamics of her high school, she described how there was a club for "finding" and spreading kindness, except "the irony of that was just no one there was the kindest individual. Everyone was just so fake to your face." She spoke extensively about the "toxicity" of her high school experience and how that impacted her mentally.

Caprielle mentioned that while she was new to her high school, she came in as a "ray of sunshine," initially forming friendships with the "popular girls." She felt like her positivity made way for many of her new classmates to gravitate towards her, and she came in optimistically because her older sisters also had close friends from the school, and their younger siblings were Caprielle's age, which could have provided the opportunity to make an easier transition. Yet, when her "shine diminished" because of some personal challenges, the change in the response she got from others seemed drastic. No longer did she have people reaching out or walking with her to class. Without getting into too much detail, Caprielle said, "[It] just affected my mental health even more, losing all these people that I was starting a relationship with."

Looking back, Caprielle saw that she didn't really want to be part of the social group she had started to befriend:

> You see a person face to face, and you're nice but kind of submissive or passive. And then behind your back, you don't get included, or they talk about you badly, or you're judged. And that was my experience. I was in the popular group, I guess you could say, but I never actually fit in. I just sat with them at lunch, or I just talked with them during my classes, but I never hung out with them outside of school. And it just grew to be this really toxic thing for mental health and my academics.

Yet, she acknowledged how the structure and culture of her private school experience were conducive to and encouraged behavior like that:

But besides that, the private high school that I went to, I guess, draws in those kinds of people where it was in a zip code that had a pretty high income, so you're surrounded by all these kids [who] . . . get like Ferraris for their birthdays, or like these massive big, big differences that I could just not really fathom or relate to in that sense.

Overall, Caprielle grew to realize that her peers weren't people she wanted to connect with, which made it easier for her to pursue alternative educational pathways in the latter half of high school. For her, the isolation of pandemic lockdowns meant freedom from this unproductive peer environment, allowing her to refocus her energy on learning through a fully online dual-enrollment option (discussed more in another chapter).

Eddie: "It just all seemed sort of fake to me."

Like Caprielle, Eddie also found that going to school online helped him avoid social dynamics about high school that he didn't particularly like. For him, pandemic lockdowns started at the end of his sophomore year, and then in the beginning of his junior year, he had the option to go in person or to continue online. He described how all the added barriers of constant testing, masking, and distancing, combined with the fact that he "really didn't like school," meant that there for him "wasn't a lot of motivation to go in person."

This interest in being online was in part because he felt he "learned more, to be honest," when taking his classes online:

I like to do my own research when it comes to things I don't know. [And] I was doing football at the time, so I still got to see the people I wanted to see. Plus, most of the social stuff—I don't

> *know; [I've] graduated now, and nobody talks to anybody else anymore. I'm kind of glad I didn't invest so much in that aspect. It wasn't much of a loss to me . . . . It's like everybody's just acting a certain way because they have to. . . . It all just seemed sort of fake to me. . . . A lot of people, which is understandable, were pretty sad during lockdown, [but] I was getting stuff done, and I feel like I work better when I'm alone. . . . So, it was almost like it helped me, if anything, to be free of having to uphold a certain facade.*

Eddie then went on to describe how not putting energy into that social facade meant he had the energy and time to accomplish the plan described in the family chapter: stacking up all his junior and senior core requirements into his junior year and completing them all online. This freed him up to do all applied electives in person on a partner campus his senior year, electives that created his most engaging learning experiences, described in more detail in other chapters.

Grace: "I had to change to a 'lower-level' class so I could actually learn."

For Grace, the first time she had to make really deliberate choices about how her peers would influence her learning came in her first year of university:

> *If I am being honest, the element of peers competing with each other was somewhat surprising to me. I wasn't exposed to a high-pressure, competitive approach to education until I entered college. Maybe it was the general nature of support and community encouragement that was the hallmark of the majority-minority, low-income student population in my high school, but I never felt like I was seriously competing with strangers*

while there. However, I noticed a dramatic shift once I was at an "elite" institution. Students here call it "Penn face," this pressure many students feel to act as if they already know everything they need to know, have no questions, and are above the need for help and support.

Penn is not the only competitive institution this occurs at; one of our colleagues who has worked with students at Northwestern University says there students call it "Northwestern face."

Grace first noticed how students seemed to feel the need to treat class as a place to show they already knew everything rather than a place to learn, make mistakes, and ask questions in her first week at Penn:

Students not only weren't asking questions, [but] I could overhear them talking on the first day about how they already knew all the content and how well they'd do in class. Chemistry 101 was a large, lecture-style course (about 120–180 students), and I quickly realized that I wouldn't be able to form deep relationships with my professor or my peers and that it would inhibit me from feeling comfortable asking the kinds of questions that would actually help me learn. So, even though I had qualified for this higher level of chemistry, I went to my academic adviser and asked to switch to Chemistry 100. It was a much smaller class (max of 40 students) where none of the students thought they were already good at chemistry—they admitted their anxieties about this STEM course. They expected to find it hard, and the professor made a point of forming a relationship with students to help us. We met a couple times a week, each lecture lasting a couple of hours, with breaks in between. The course was structured so that there were more practice problems integrated into the lecture, which gave more opportunities to practice and learn in real-time.

Grace had to change to a "lower-level" class so she could actually learn—not because the content of the higher class was too hard for her, but because the peer dynamics were so unproductive.

As Grace got to know students in other competitive schools, she came to realize that "at many so-called elite schools, almost everyone is jealous of someone else." She recounted:

Even if they're not using the word "jealous," they're most certainly comparing themselves to someone else in a way that hurts themselves or others in the comparison. It discouraged me to realize that right at the moment when we could benefit most from supporting each other through very challenging academic demands, instead, my peers felt like they had to act as if they were so superior and well-equipped that they didn't need the kind of genuine connection that only happens when we're honest and vulnerable with each other.

She was glad that she "could at least choose a different course environment, where that peer performance wouldn't have such a negative effect" on her learning.

Grace's realization that being surrounded by peers who were invested in learning over performance deepened further when she participated in a summer research program[28] just before starting her sophomore university year. She remembers clearly how one of the older undergrads told her, "Your sophomore year is when your friendships will change the most."

Grace frowned. "Really?" she asked.

Grace was working on a project edwith her new friend, Sophia, who was a senior at another local university, when they started reflecting on Sophia's time as an undergrad. She mentioned that many of her friendships changed and solidified during her sophomore year because "that's when people change."

"But don't people 'change' every year in college?" Grace asked.

"Exactly," Sophia replied. "But it's especially so during your sophomore year."

Grace described how she "internalized this moment because it was a flash point for how [her] approach to making and maintaining friendships post-COVID changed." She added, "Possibly this reflection is also representative of the change between making and maintaining friendships from high school to college, but I would be remiss if I ignored the impact of COVID on how my generation makes meaningful friendships inside and outside of the classroom":

Soon after graduation, and while COVID was coming to an "end," I had moved to a new state where students were moving back on campus. But, I didn't have strong friendships or support my first year on campus. Nearly every day, I made the dreaded 15-minute trek back home from my evening General Chemistry course that was held on the other side of campus, making a conscious decision to ignore the bustling socializing groups of students around me by phoning a friend of mine in Texas or family members back home in Maryland. This walk always made me feel lonely, an outsider, and a social and academic imposter on the campus of an Ivy League university that was often characterized as the "Social Ivy"—everyone seemed to have an active social life despite their busy and strenuous academic schedules. I felt isolated from my peers on campus, so rather than seeking out friends there, I turned back to the people I already knew and could keep in touch with remotely. As a direct result, I found myself being more closed off to friendships that could've helped during my transition into college life.

As Grace recalled her reaction to feeling like an outsider, she began to wonder if something similar was happening to other students:

Were they also just responding with walls to protect themselves after coming off the combination of lockdown isolation and starting up a new life in a challenging environment? Was this the ouroboros of "Penn Face," with each of us stuck pretending we were fine while actually feeling lost, because we thought that was what we were supposed to do? Or are some of us so focused on our goals and aspirations that we forget simple courtesies—either intentionally or unintentionally—and everyone around us seems to fall by the wayside?

Regardless of the cause, she really had to work to find connections on campus during her first year of undergrad.

Fortunately, when Grace did the SUMR program, she found making connections much easier, "particularly because many of them were upperclassmen and [they] already felt comfortable in their own right." She shared how:

It seemed as though there was no reason for "competition" since everyone was in the program to learn something from each other. I was pleasantly surprised to have found genuinely kind and down-to-earth scholars from Penn and other universities—who contrasted the seemingly superficial, aggressively ambitious, and emotional immaturity of what I knew from my first couple of semesters at Penn. I remain close with many of them to this day. They are the reason why I feel more socially and emotionally supported and secure at Penn. They are the reason why I feel more secure in my abilities to be a better person and learner inside and outside of the classroom, and I feel more open to making deeper friendships. I am striving every day to break down any "Penn Face" I've unconsciously picked up so that I can find and connect with the people who are a good fit for me.

As Grace reflected on Sophia's comment that sophomore year shows the greatest change in friendships, she felt especially glad to have participated in the summer program:

It's not to say I had no friends my first year or that the connections I made that year weren't satisfying, but I could not maintain many of those friendships. If not for the summer program, I would've entered my second year in university feeling like I had to stick with the connections that I made as a freshman, without realizing that there is a natural ebb and flow in friendships and friendly acquaintances, which is a more common experience than most young people realize.

Grace came to the conclusion that not only did "finding friends who had nothing to prove" help her with her learning, but it was also "the start of my journey of navigating friendships as a young adult."

King: "If they can't welcome you, it's not a you problem."

Unfortunately, many of the students we spoke with were in environments where some element of their identity was not welcomed—usually related to race, sexuality, and/or gender. As a result, they experienced bullying from their peers for the ways in which they didn't fit the "norm," and they had to sometimes make high-stakes choices about how to respond to or avoid those kinds of socially toxic environments.

King, for example, was a Black student in a suburb in the Northeast where almost all of his peers and his teachers were White. As mentioned in the previous chapter, the ways he was treated eventually led him to switch to homeschooling. But while he was still in public school, he had multiple experiences of being harassed due to his race. He shared one example:

I was on a bus, and we were getting ready to go home. And one kid turned to me and said the N-word to me . . . and just kept on saying it; like, it went from one person to two people saying it, and then three people started saying it, and they [all] just started saying it. And I go home, I tell my parents, [and they call the school]. And the administration, they chalk it up as "Oh, they weren't saying the N-word. They were trying to say Niger, which is a country in Africa, and they were learning it in Spanish [class]."[29]

The fact that kids and teens are often cruel to each other as they scramble for social status and their own identity isn't surprising. But that predictability makes it no less painful for the young people on the receiving end of it, especially when the school administrators acted as if the behavior was innocuous.

Repeated experiences like this, along with the more subtle feeling of exclusion caused by King not fitting in with the norms that surrounded him, began to add up, making both peers and adults in his school system untrustworthy to King and his family. He recalled that at one point, a couple of years before his interview, he came home from school having covered his skin in white marker. He described it this way:

Basically, [I was] trying to rub the black off my skin with white marker. And I look back at that like, "What made me want to do that?" Because now, if anyone knows me, they would know I love my black skin. So why would I ever want to rub it … off and try to put that white marker on me? It just sounds so crazy now, but back then I did it … because [you] see all these White people, and you're like, well, to fit in, just grab the marker. But it's not that; it's not you. If they can't welcome you, then it's not a you problem. It's a them problem. They can't accept what you got.

This also applied to his body image around his size. While in school, he described going through a phase where he was wearing "baggy clothes" all the time, refusing to ever wear shorts, even in the gym. Now, two years out from being in this school where he felt so separate from his peers, he feels far more comfortable in his body. As he put it, "This year, I love myself; I love who I've become." Getting out of that hostile environment was necessary for him to develop a sense of his identity that he felt good about.

Sometimes, Changing Focus is Enough

Obviously, it's not often feasible to completely change school environments—many families can't homeschool for a range of reasons, there aren't always online or dual-enrollment options publicly available, and some students wouldn't thrive in those options even when they are available. For Goose and Layla, changing environments wasn't feasible, so they had to find other ways to manage negative experiences with friends and classmates that initially made staying engaged in school really hard.

Goose: "I was suddenly an afterthought."

In other chapters, we discuss Goose's mostly positive experiences navigating relationships with teachers and the adults in her life. Those experiences were in sharp contrast to what happened with Goose's group of friends in her senior year of high school:

> By October, already I felt like I didn't have the friends I always thought I had, and so I suddenly started facing isolation, feeling left out. People purposely not inviting me to things, being forgotten about. It still is hard to think back on that because on one hand, who cares about what they think? [But] when it's people that ... I've known for all my life, or at least a good chunk of my education, it really sucks because you want to be able to spend time with them and have these good last few memories with them. But this year, I wasn't really offered the opportunity.

Why? As Goose put it, "Once I started being vocal about not liking some of the things they were saying or the way they were behaving, that's when I noticed that everyone dropped me, and I was suddenly an afterthought." She had specifically confronted the larger group of friends she hung out with for the way they had treated one of the other women in their group: repeatedly cracking jokes about how that person was going to get date-raped at a party, to the point that her friend started to have nightmares about it. But when Goose told them the joking should stop, they told her she was taking the whole situation too seriously and then stopped hanging out with her.

The feeling of isolation was compounded by the fact that most of the students in her high school came from wealth, which meant that she didn't feel she fit in enough to find other peers to connect with in her final year when she was dropped by her core friend group. She explained that she just "[doesn't] speak" when she's around these peers:

When you're surrounded by those types of people who, every day, they're talking about what colleges they want to go to and how much help they're getting, they start talking about all the country clubs they go to, and they talk about how they visit each other's houses. Sometimes, they even compare wealth amongst each other.

For Goose, being in a public school district with a lot of wealthy families, while she herself didn't come from wealth, was both awkward and stifling. This contributed to her decision to focus on just finishing up her final year of high school and on getting out to somewhere where she might be able to find friends who shared her values and understood her experiences rather than trying to make new friends once she'd realized her existing group of friends wasn't as solid as she'd thought it was.

Layla: "Why can't you measure up?"

Layla also experienced being excluded by her core group of friends, though for different reasons than Goose's. For Layla, the exclusion arose when she stumbled, emotionally and academically, after a breakup. Layla and her then-boyfriend had initially been quite close, both as children of highly driven immigrant parents. Many first-generation young students of immigrant parents can connect on one of the more pressing matters of their childhood. It didn't matter to their parents whether they were chosen last to play dodgeball or if they didn't get what they wanted to eat at lunchtime; it was the constant pressure to "be better," starting with achieving straight A's from grade school on.

This was something Layla and her boyfriend could both relate to, and they built a connection. But when they entered college and Layla was struggling with school, there seemed to be a constant slight pressure from her then-boyfriend to push herself harder and succeed more quickly. "I didn't even realize how quick[ly] I could fail. It makes sense in high school because each assignment adds up piece by piece. But this is just like two assignments, [and] you're [already failing]," Layla recalled. "And it really hurts because I was just like, 'Am I broken? Why can everybody do it but me?' I really felt so alone."

Like Grace experienced at a different university, peer pressure to act successful was also part of Layla's campus culture, despite some students occasionally talking about their struggles. When they did, Layla noticed they still did so in a competitive way:

I don't know one person [who's] confessed about how they felt and honestly truly meant it without still feeling better than someone else. I feel like they're thinking, "Bottom line, at least

I'm not the worst at my school.". . . Because it's like it's a general consensus that we all understand what we're doing, but also that we're all a little bit better than the others, like this general elitist feeling . . . like the minute you speak up, it's like you've fallen down, like you don't know. And you can even ask and not get the answer but still get . . . that condescension.

This environment of competition and judgmental comparison not only made it hard for her to ask questions when confused in class, but it also made it hard for Layla to seek out the help she needed academically and personally.

Additionally, this sense of competition was amplified by her then-boyfriend. At one point, he said that he was working harder than her. She understood that he had experienced similar pressures to succeed from his mother, but she couldn't accept the same pressures from him. For Layla, this was a struggle; it felt like "we have to be top tier together." These pressures made Layla feel inadequate and "stupid," a feeling that she had already subconsciously felt for months. This conflict led to their breakup.

In this same week, she had been diagnosed with ADHD, anxiety, and depression. Soon after, Layla attempted suicide. These subsequent events—the diagnoses, school pressures, and break-up—were tipping points, but it was ultimately the more abstract feeling of being lost that lingered.

As she tried to regain her mental and emotional footing after her suicide attempt, Layla turned to the peers she thought of as friends, but they sometimes avoided her, and when they saw her, they changed the subject of conversation. Initially, Layla was confused about why they weren't responding with the support she wanted. "It felt so denouncing. I wasn't allowed to speak about my ex or anything about my grades or ADHD or anything, all these new things I just found out about myself." Eventually, she confronted them and, in that confrontation, realized that while she had thought of them as close friends, they had thought of her simply as an acquaintance. This added to her feelings of aimlessness. "I woke up [and] I didn't even know what to do, like my day-to-day routine. I didn't know if I should get breakfast or coffee or should I study, because when you have no schedule, you really have nothing to do, but you have work to do. And I just procrastinated all day, weeks on weeks."

Then, "something in me just broke. I went on a crying spree for like two days, and I couldn't understand why I was crying." But after that:

I just started studying. I don't know if that makes sense. I just started studying when I woke up and then after lunch, and then it became a repetitive motion of waking up every day [to] wash my face, brush my teeth, take my meds, and then [study]. I had to force such a consistent schedule. I had a 6% in calculus, and I just finished with a 73%, and I'm so happy.

This shift from orienting to success metrics from others to acknowledging what a win looked like to her made a huge difference in her ability to stay engaged in school. Layla realized that she could make choices that helped her feel better without needing the approval of her peers or her boyfriend to get those feelings.

Because teens' brains are shifting to make them care about the approval of their peers so much more than they did before, it can make it especially hard to find another way to stay motivated without that sense of belonging in school. For Caprielle, Eddie, Grace, King, Goose, and Layla, it took jarring and unusual events to prompt them to change their environments or their strategies. Seeing where they still had real choices they could make and acting on those options restored their confidence in their ability to succeed in school.

But the Ideal Is When Friendships Strengthen Learning

Beyond the specific challenges shared above by interviewees, the current generation of young people has had to weather significant challenges to forming and sustaining meaningful friendships (between the effects of social media and the effects of the pandemic). Despite these challenges, however, some interviewees talked about how much of a positive difference having friends in school made for their learning (and their lives). Whether it was casual classroom friendships that made it easier to learn or having deeper connections, learning was easier when done with friends.

Melanie, Avery, and Grace: Having friends in class makes it easier to engage.

Most interviewees made offhand remarks about how having friends in class made it easier to engage. Melanie, Avery, and Grace each gave a few examples of how this was the case. "I think what was honestly really important to make my classes engaging were to have peers in it that I was friends with that I was willing to talk to," Melanie said. "I've been very lucky all four years of high school to have friends in my classes, and kind of like my best friends in almost all my classes." In the occasional class without friends, "it was much more difficult to engage with the teachers and with the curriculum [because] I didn't have anyone to talk to when I had a question, or [a way] to study together. So, there's that lack of motivation, [and that] was definitely an issue."

Avery shared a similar example. "I [had] more friends within my chemistry class, which obviously makes it more interesting and entertaining. Having a good relationship with friends and teachers definitely makes everything, just school in general, much easier—looking forward to certain classes, your lunch, [any time] when I see my friends." Sometimes, it was more than just someone to look forward to:

With my math class in particular, though, if I don't understand something, there is another kid in the class who will re-explain it to me with simpler language. Because my math teacher will use terms that he thinks we'll understand, but I don't understand a lot of them, which gets me confused, and when I'm confused, I don't pay attention. So, if I don't understand something, I'll ask the other kid in my class who is very helpful, and he'll explain it to me, and I'll get it pretty easily.

Avery was very grateful that this friend was willing to help him out in this way during the open work times in class or in the hallways just after class had ended.

Similarly, Grace grew to appreciate the value of those kinds of classmate friends as she got into the more convoluted, large lecture-style courses at Penn. Grace realized she had taken them for granted in high school:

In high school classes, I always knew someone who ran in similar friend circles as I did, so if I didn't know them well, at least I knew someone who knew them. This was enough. In a large university, however, I could no longer expect a friend would just happen to already be in whatever class I was taking. I noticed how much it affected me when I realized I went from feeling isolated and deeply concerned about how I might not be able to succeed in my organic chemistry class to feeling a tremendous sense of relief when I saw a friend come in through the lecture hall doors. She was someone I had taken a previous General Chemistry course with, so I knew we had similar experiences with enduring a complex science course. Knowing I had someone I could study and talk about confusing lectures with, without worrying that they'd be judging my shortcomings, made the class feel far more manageable. She wasn't simply a casual friend who I'd passively say hi to; she was someone I could be vulnerable with, and I continued to nurture our friendship throughout the class. It was comforting having a friend I could go to for assurance about everything from simple homework questions to more intimate stories about our experiences with school.

Grace realized later how that experience made her enjoy Organic Chemistry "a lot more than [she] realized," and she and that other student are "still close friends to this day."

Elena: "It was good camaraderie because everybody wanted to be there."

Elena attended a rigorous summer art program, where she met and connected with peers who shared her passion for art. This was especially important to her because the schools she's been in haven't had art electives or school-based extracurriculars that allowed her to go deeply into that interest. So, she began participating in contests and opportunities outside her school, including the Portfolio Plus Program at Washington University, an intensive summer program that she loved. She described it as "the most academic art program you could dream up. . . . We had to write short essays about our work, and then deeply critique our peers with supporting claims and stuff like that, and then also analyze the contemporary artworks that we were given [to study]."

For Elena, this program "was the first time [she] had studied contemporary art," which also made it more interesting to her. She also talked about how the fact that "it was in a studio setting" and that she "was with other people [her] age who were also equally serious and very engaged in art" made the whole thing "just a really cool experience." This led to "good camaraderie because everybody wanted to be there. . . .

Everybody was quite good. They had different skill levels, but I also got to learn from [them], especially during critique sessions. And that was new for me."

She kept in contact with the friends she made in the program, and the program helped her verify whether or not she was interested in pursuing an art-related major in college before getting to college. In other words, this extracurricular pursuit had an amazing combination of wins for her, not only allowing her to find peers she could belong with through their shared passions but also furthering her abilities and goals and giving her the chance to make choices not available to her at school.

Vivian and King: Meaningful conversations and safe spaces

Sometimes it's possible to find peers to connect with and learn from in extracurriculars that are actually at school. This was the case for Vivian, a 16-year-old junior at a suburban public high school in the mid-Atlantic, who described herself as Asian American. She joined a student-led county-wide program aimed at closing the opportunity gap:

> All of these meetings are run by students, typically upperclassmen. . . . And so, during these meetings, they would often bring up some topic [sparked by] . . . real events that have occurred in real life. And then sometimes they'll use that as a segway into whatever content that they will be discussing. And it's often content that includes social issues, issues of equity. And then what really drew me into [this program] was afterward they would open the floor up for discussion. And this was, it wasn't just like a lecture, because I don't think I would be as engaged if I just sat there to listen to, you know, like, five upperclassmen lecture me on something. No, they would open up the floor for people like me, even if I wasn't that knowledgeable about the topic,

to just share my opinion, and share my thoughts, and maybe bring up something else that's kind of related to that. And then the conversation would just continue. And this was the reason I was so engaged with [this program], because of the conversations that we would have. And it would be conversations about, you know, these heavy topics; it would be conversations that were really productive. It was really good for people to explain their thoughts and share how they felt about certain issues, how it relates to their life, how they see it in their school, how they see it in the media, how they see it in life, and just to have that continuous conversation.

These meaningful discussions not only made Vivian feel like she belonged, even as a newcomer, but they did so in a way that built her abilities (to understand and talk about difficult topics like equity).

As Vivian got more involved in this program and started participating in county-wide events, meaningful peer discussions also allowed her to develop a new and unexpected appreciation for the dynamics at her school:

So, when I was at the internship and I was speaking with these interns, who were all students of color who go to these high schools that are predominantly White institutions, they're often the only person of color, or one of like three people of color, in their class. [And they would] speak about really scary racial incidents that have happened at their school, and I'm used to feeling like I always have to defend [my] high school whenever I'm in a setting with students from other high schools because we get a really bad reputation. But when I was at this internship, I was like, dang, [our] high school, we're doing great. Like, we don't have these really racist incidents happening at our school. So, I felt really privileged in a way to attend [my] high school, a majority-minority school that gets a really bad reputation. Because I've never felt like my identity was under such a scary attack.

The positive difference it made to be in a school where she and her peers shared a diverse range of racial and ethnic backgrounds wasn't something Vivian had seen as an asset prior to hearing these stories about other schools, and it gave her something new to appreciate about her high school. It also flipped on its head the typical narrative about her high school in her county, where it was usually discussed as a "bad" school because of its low test scores and large minority population.

King had a somewhat similar realization when he left his primarily White school district to begin homeschooling and he began to spend more of his time with other Black students as a result. This increase in peer support was deeply helpful to him. As he described it, "It feels very, very good to know that, in any time of crisis, you could call on people who know you . . . and who have probably been through similar stuff as you, because almost every Black person has dealt with racism at least once." For both Vivian and King, it was meaningful to realize what an asset it could be to have peers who not only didn't harass each other for who they were, but also inherently understood and could offer support.

What to Do to Support Positive Peer Dynamics

The fact that it can be normal for high school and college students to experience a lot of social upheaval from their peers can make it very challenging to know how to support young people in this arena. The likelihood that they even want help from adults is already low in the first place, and some kinds of intervention are more likely to do harm than good (being a "snowplow" parent deprives young people of both choice and voice, and it's easy to imagine how an awkward social situation could rapidly worsen with parental involvement, for example). However, some of the most painful peer experiences interviewees shared were the ones when a student was seeking support, adults were involved, and the adults didn't help—like Layla's parents suggesting she just study less or the school administrators who defended King's peers with a shoddy excuse.

In other words, there is a role for adults to play in young people's peer dynamic *sometimes*, but knowing when and how to do so is tricky. The stories shared above illustrate two important paths for responding to negative situations—listening deeply when your help is requested, especially when there's a real risk of harm, and, where possible, collaborating on what action to take rather than jumping straight to your own decision. Nurturing positive peer relationships and environments and decreasing the impact of the bad ones is subtle work. Since students didn't have much advice on this, we turned to some experienced practitioners for the strategies they've seen work, and those ideas are shared below.

More Ideas From Experienced Practitioners

For Families:

- Knowing that, during teenage years, both emotions and the importance of peer relationships are heightened, show your child unconditional support if they are having a tough time with peers. Don't minimize it. It is (and should be, from a developmental perspective) a big deal to them. The intensity of these relationships is very real and fully felt by the young person; invalidating that emotional intensity can feel like rejection. Students may need help with retaining balance between the emotional intensity of interpersonal relationships and the other areas of their lives, but this will only succeed if the importance and intensity are acknowledged and respected.

- Encourage young people to nurture a small number of close, true friendships with peers who are kind, as opposed to trying to fit in with full groups or with peers who make them feel bad.

- Be aware that bullying occurs even between "friends" and that your teen may not realize they don't deserve that treatment or that it's reflective of an issue from that "friend" rather than something wrong with them.

- Adults can also help shift the tone of these relationships by reinforcing a student's idea of self-concept, for example, by having the student reflect on their own values.

- It can sometimes be very complicated to navigate the educational system when discriminatory or bullying interactions are happening. Parents and teachers should ask about and listen to students' concerns about how any information they present may be handled and respond accordingly. For example, if a student explains that a guidance counselor chronically denies overt racism, parents talking to that guidance counselor will likely be an exercise in futility and may require reaching out to the vice principal, principal, or superintendent (armed with the information of how that interaction was unsuccessful). Or, for example, when the idea of changing schools because of bullying within a district is shut down by a student because on social media, "everyone there knows anyways," that student is likely telling you the truth, and you may need to fight for a different option, such as going outside of that district.

- Remind students that in certain circumstances, parents, teachers, and administrators will intervene because of school policy or safety. It may also be worth reminding them that they are not mental health professionals and that if they are acutely worried about someone's safety, they should involve trusted adults right away.

For Educators:

- Don't overlook the effect of the peer culture in your classroom and your school. While it may be hard to do something to change it, it's still better to visibly try and fall short than to just let cruelty stand unchallenged.

- Create opportunities for students to get to know each other one-on-one in class (not just in school-sponsored events after hours, which not all families can participate in), with safe but thought-provoking exchanges that can build their curiosity and connection with each other. The students will end up learning more if they have peers they feel connected with in class, so it isn't wasted time.

Supporting Choices, Building Abilities, and Making It All Relevant

4

Using Their Voice

Making Choices In and Outside the Classroom

"Student problems are just adult problems for younger people. . . . Just because they're young doesn't mean that they . . . aren't facing real serious issues in their day-to-day lives. So, acknowledge that and understand that students have their own lives, thoughts, and opinions . . . and deserve to be treated with respect and empathy. That doesn't go away just because they're young. A lot of them do bring a lot of intelligence and wisdom and do care a lot about their education, whether they show it or not. At the end of the day, it's hard not to care about something you're spending 40 hours a week or more doing. . . . Oftentimes, parents feel disconnected from their kids, and a lot of teachers feel similarly, but just working with [students] first and coming from a place of not wanting to lecture and immediately make change but a place to really hear them out and understand . . . is your step zero to fixing a lot of the problems you see in education. . . . Talk to them, ask what they're thinking about and worried about, what they're spending their time doing and why, and if they do care. Because oftentimes, when students say they don't care, they actually do care a lot; it's just not about the thing they think you're asking about. . . . Hearing students out and letting them use their voice and right to respect themselves is one of the most powerful things you can do."

- Connor

"Facilitate change. Where you dislike if you feel something is inad-equate, perhaps do something yourself, perhaps suggest it to some-one in the administration, whatever, do something. Even if it doesn't work, it makes you feel better."

- Zimo

Abilities, belonging, and choices all work together to make it possible to sustain motivation. We focused on belonging first because having a foundation of connection and safety makes it possible to be curious, open, and receptive to learning new skills and mindsets and to identifying and pursuing meaningful choices. As the previous chapters show, positive relationships with families, teachers, and peers often create meaningful opportunities for teens to make choices that matter to them and to strengthen or discover abilities they value. Abilities, belonging, and choices all affect each other so much that it's hard to talk about one without also discussing the others. However, the stories in this chapter focus first on the choices students made, whether about mindsets, classes, programs, or extracurriculars, and how those choices affected their experience of school.

Choosing How to Respond

Later in this chapter, we'll look at the two most common ways students can exert autonomy over their high school and college experience: by choosing what they do inside their classes and what they do outside those classes. Students we spoke with made it clear, over and over again, that they wished they had pushed themselves to find places where they could make meaningful choices earlier and figured out how to act on those opportunities. However, not all students have the same level of choices available in or outside of class. While the structures and relationships that surround students affect just how much autonomy they actually have, there is one way everyone always has a choice—deciding their response to what happens to them.

Ava: "Even though the comments hurt me, I make a point to forget about it."

Like Tuesday and King, Ava experienced unwelcoming and racist remarks in her rural school, and she had to decide how she wanted to handle it. She described instances where students made anti-Asian jokes at her expense. Comments that resembled a certain stereotype, such as saying her lunch must have contained cat meat or snarkily asking if she could "really be Asian" after she got less than an A on a math test. She described her reactions to these jokes: "Usually I play it off, but honestly, it hurts. Especially since it's always the same overused jokes. And . . . I don't really show [the hurt] because my school was predominantly White, and if you can't take the joke, you're not cool, or you're 'sensitive.'" Ava didn't want to deal with the repercussions of having to defend herself *by herself,* so she acted like the jokes were fine: a form of uncomfortable self-defense most people who have been the butt of ridicule, especially racially charged ridicule, can relate to.

These experiences were worsened by the fact that teachers didn't do anything to stop the racist remarks from occurring "even though they heard it. [Sometimes] teachers would [say], 'Oh, that's so mean of you to say,' but they never stopped it, ever."

> *Grace: Do you still feel engaged in that classroom after the teacher hasn't stepped in to say anything? Does your relationship with that teacher change?*
>
> *Ava: Honestly, no. I don't know why. But even though the comments hurt me, I make a point to forget about it. Just because, honestly, I don't really know why. I just feel like it wouldn't be*

very beneficial for me if I disengage from talking to those people or learning from those teachers because I feel like it's just how they—here, it's the normal. And there's not much I can do as a person to change it. Because . . . there are probably two Asians throughout my entire school. And [my peers] don't really understand, and I see that they're brought up that way. There's a lot of ignorance going around.

For many people, this would be an almost supernatural level of calm—to assess that it wouldn't benefit her to "disengage" from her classes, to see the context for why the people are treating her that way, and to decide that, for her at least, trying to change the environment is just not worth it.

For students who were able to get involved in coordinated efforts for equity advocacy—like Vivian and Ian, who advocated for equity in their schools via their extracurricular activities—pushing to make positive change in their schools and communities was meaningful and energizing. But for a student like Ava, where the school environment and lack of allies within it made it such an uphill battle to make change, choosing to ignore these remarks was the best solution. Additionally, she sought out extracurricular opportunities to escape this unwelcoming environment, which are described more in a few pages.

Tuesday: "Notice how things are right now, without judgment."

As discussed elsewhere, Tuesday found himself in a similarly unwelcoming environment, where neither the school nor his parents accepted him as a trans man and where his peers also often mocked him for his Asian features and larger body. Like Ava, he found one of the few places he could make choices was in his response to these situations, since he didn't have enough support to change how people treated him. Tuesday pursued professional mental health support because of this environment, including checking himself into inpatient mental health facilities:

Teaching coping skills in general [in school] would be amazing, but specifically radical acceptance, so that when people are stressed out, they just could sit down and let go of this illusion of control. And notice that things are how things are right now, without judgment. And I think that [radical acceptance] also . . . teaches people to just generally be non-judgmental, and to . . . see things from both sides of the coin. . . . Dialectical Behavior Therapy is just about making sure people see both sides to everything.

Obviously, any teacher who isn't also a licensed mental health care professional wouldn't be qualified to lead classes in Dialectical Behavior Therapy, and there can be risks to mandating it in the classroom.[30] However, the concepts that Tuesday wishes he'd learned in school aren't exclusive to that form of therapy—coping skills for stress, seeing things from multiple perspectives, and mindfully observing "how things are right now" are crucial to many good SEL programs that schools can invest in. And for students in schools who aren't doing useful programs, finding a like-minded community to join locally or even using free mindfulness resources available through apps and websites can be a way to explore and practice these skills.

Caprielle: "Finding joy in the little things."

Caprielle had one main piece of advice for younger students who were seeking to make their school experience better:

Last summer, I really learned to find joy in the little things, and as much as that seems very cliche, it really helped me... I feel like that's what human existence is. It's really about finding things to get us through every day. And although that sounds probably depressing, I think that mindset can really help people like it did for me. I would watch the rain fall... and I'd think, "I just really love the sound of rain" or "I really like watering my plants." I just found that finding the little things was always such a big help for me. So, in terms of [younger students] going into high school, as one of my favorite quotes goes, "expect nothing and appreciate everything." I learned, since I was ousted from the popular group, to take the rejection as a redirection and instead use the time to grow into a better version of myself. I found that nine years at the same elementary/middle school went by in a blip, so I hope four years of high school easily passes [for] both me and younger students, too.

Caprielle is referencing how the "popular" girls she had originally been friends with dropped her once she became less sunny and bubbly in response to some difficult things that were happening in her life. This strategy was one she developed after that happened, and it allowed her to look at her high school experience differently, with greater distance and less distress.

Grace and Melanie: Focusing on school can be a helpful way to counterbalance stress at home.

Similar to Caprielle, Grace tries to maintain a more optimistic perspective, though it took her a while to find a healthy balance in how to do it:

In my sophomore year of high school, I learned my parents were getting divorced. In my head, I strongly believed that if I focused on the time allotted to me, in a day, in a week, months, and years, then I would remember that in the "grand scheme" of my life, this stressor of my parents' divorce was a small blot. I remember writing in my journal: "This moment where you are struggling is temporary, fleeting. This momentary struggle will pass away. It won't last forever." I want to emphasize that this isn't to say that my, or anyone else's, struggles are not valid, but it helped me to focus on my life from a top-down perspective and use school as both a distraction and a haven.

Unfortunately, there are healthy ways of redirecting attention and ways that aren't so healthy, and initially, Grace started to fall into the latter. Looking back, she wished she had relied more on the people around her for support.

Initially, Grace didn't tell any friends about what was happening in her life, trying to deal with the stress in other ways:

I opted to emotionally isolate myself and take on more responsibility than I could handle at school. As a result, I ended up creating unhealthy habits as a form of distraction: I skipped meals and slept late in order to be "productive." I developed incapacitating migraines, which only further contributed to my desire to sleep less in order to "catch up" on my productivity. But later that year, COVID-19 had spread to the States, and we were on lockdown. I was fortunate enough to be able to use the space and unstructured time lockdown created to focus on my mental and physical health and figure out a routine that worked best for my health first and school second. I scheduled more time to take daily morning walks with my family, getting sunlight and fresh air, eating three structured and appropriately sized meals a day, taking vitamins, and, most importantly, sleeping enough. I ensured that I made choices about my health before I incorporated school and classes into my day.

As a result of these changes, Grace was able to figure out better coping skills. "I continue to use these skills today so that I can get what I want and need out of school without being obsessed with hyperproductivity."

Similarly, Melanie and her family experienced a significant amount of stress. Unlike Grace, Melanie sought out a few friends and trusted adults to connect with, as described in prior chapters. She also chose school as a productive place to focus her attention during stressful times at home and found that helped her manage that stress:

> I felt like I needed to remove myself from the situation and try to find something else to occupy my time and my mind. So, I dove into school. And also, I didn't want to worry my parents, [I thought] "This is my job, to do school while they're dealing with that [Melanie's mom's cancer treatments]." That was the best I could do. So yeah, I think it was fine, but it was definitely often difficult during those years.

This conscious decision also set her up to have mental clarity when things got stressful again in high school after her mother read her diary and discovered she was queer. As Melanie put it, "When I'm stressed, I just like to do calculus, and it makes everything feel better." Melanie laughed when she said this, saying, "Yeah, just super nerdy," in a self-effacing way, but the strategy of choosing something to develop mastery over when there are other things out of one's control isn't only available for self-proclaimed "nerds"—it can work in non-academic areas too. Melanie herself also focused her energy on non-academic areas as well, like wildlife photography (see her story in the extracurriculars section for more details).

Choosing Teachers, Classes, and Programs

While it's easy to notice all the seemingly immoveable requirements of high school that inhibit choice, it's possible to find options that can make a real difference even without over-hauling the educational system. Just looking for where it's possible to make more choices builds a sense of autonomy—for example, learning about which teachers to seek out, which electives to opt into, and whether there are optional programs (like dual-enrollment or vo-tech) through which to earn high school credits. Oftentimes, options like these aren't well-advertised, but they provide significantly more opportunities for students to have agency over their high school experience.

Tuesday and Elena: Tips for "picking" your high school teachers

Two of the students we spoke with talked about specific strategies they used to make it more likely to get teachers they wanted to be in a classroom with. For example, Tuesday said, "I chose most classes in my high school career that had teachers that I liked. So, if there was a teacher I didn't like, I usually made sure not to take the class, and thankfully, my interests lined up with good teachers. . . . The one-on-one aspect was probably the best part of the rural aspect [of where I live]." The smaller, more rural community Tuesday lived in was overall not a good fit for him because his identity as a half-Chinese trans student put him at odds with many of the social norms of this community. However, the small school meant it was possible to know the teachers in advance, and having a sense of who would be a good fit meant more one-on-one attention available.

Elena talked about how she would get to know students in grade levels above her to find out more info about who were the good teachers and who were the "duds":

I was so extra, Becca—I got my counselor's email addresses, and I would write emails, but very [was] polite, bugging, and then call and leave voicemails to make sure that I would not get as many dud teachers for next year. . . . Sometimes I was really concerned that a lot of it came off as passive-aggressive, but if you didn't have an advocate at school, if your parent wasn't a teacher or a staff member at my high school, it was pretty difficult to advocate for yourself. For example, my year, we had maybe 340 seniors graduating, but I would say at least 12 of them all have faculty as their parents. And so, they used their parents to get classes.

The disparities Elena saw between what the more connected students got versus everyone else was reason enough for her to try. "I'd say my high school just suffered from lots of discrimination and small-town, local nepotism," and that made it really helpful to go to people in upper classes to "learn how the social politics of [my] individual school setting worked." Since Elena didn't experience any downsides from being "extra," she kept it up and advised other students to try the same.

Melanie and Eddie: Having a wide range of electives helps.

Melanie described her school as "pretty good because they had a lot of electives." She added:

My school offers a nursing elective class, a pharmacy elective class, a physiology class—so I took all of them in the same year. It was [during] COVID [restrictions], so it's definitely a little bit lower quality than I would have hoped for. But I definitely still learned more about topics that are still interesting to me.

We asked if her school was particularly focused on healthcare electives, and she said it had a wide range beyond that:

The school just has [lots of] electives, so this year, I took a class on civil conversation, an English elective. They have a Black history elective. They have Holocaust history. . . . They have computer science. It is just something else to help kids. I definitely commend the school. I think there's a lot of better resources than some other schools and what I had expected coming in.

Eddie's high school achieved a similarly wide range of electives by virtue of their partnerships with two other programs that were housed on a separate campus that other high schools could also work with. The range of options offered by these two programs, in a wide variety of applied topics like architecture, programming, and business, is what motivated him to push through all of his standard academic requirements in his junior year so he could exclusively take classes from these programs his senior year. For teens and parents interested in advocacy at the district level, pushing for the kind of options Melanie and Eddie had is one path worth considering.

Maria, Brian, and Ian: Choosing an alternate high school

Maria, a 16-year-old junior in a college-focused charter school in the Southwest, described herself as Latina and mentioned that her parents had immigrated to the U.S. from Mexico. She was able to make a choice about what school she attended and went to a college-prep-focused charter school. She talked about how much she appreciated the way the school helped students explore college in relation to their interests and really broke the process of preparing for college down into manageable steps.

Brian, a 19-year-old who had recently completed high school, described himself as biracial (Asian and White), on the autism spectrum, and uninterested in academic performance. He had switched from a public, in-person high school to a private, virtual high school after his first two years of high school did not go well. Whereas most students found their way into online classes due to pandemic restrictions, Brian deliberately chose to go fully virtual through a private high school, Fusion Global Academy. What he liked about the program was two elements of the flexibility it allowed him, both in the timing of classes and in the method of instruction. As he described it:

> *The environment was just more comfortable. And the way [the school] was set up, the time is much more flexible. Like, you could start classes at 12 or later. And they're also one-on-ones, so you can also discuss the topic with them, rather than it being more of a complete lecture.*

Being able to talk with his teachers one-on-one, to choose when to ask questions during lectures and about the independent classwork he was working on as those questions arose, was really helpful to Brian. He also appreciated that, when he got back graded work, he wasn't just reading the markings on his own; he could immediately talk with that teacher about their feedback if he wanted to do so.

The structure of Fusion, in other words, places a significant emphasis on student autonomy and student-teacher relationships. Obviously, this particular private program has the luxury of achieving that via a one-to-one student-to-teacher ratio, something that public schools can't afford to do. For Brian, however, this was crucial to enable him to complete his high school education; neither he nor his parents thought he would have graduated if he'd stayed in the public school he was attending initially.

Ian, a 16-year-old junior in the Northeast, described himself as Black, male, and a high-achiever with a passion for animals. Like a couple of other interviewees, he also chose the high school he attended, opting to apply to a public vocational-technical (which Ian just referred to as "vo-tech") high school that allowed him to focus on an area of study he's interested in and that even offered the option "to get all your required courses done in [the] first semester of senior year, so then you can take dual enrolled classes the high school pays for to get college credits." There were actually four vo-tech high schools to consider via a public and charter school choice program in his region, but the one he ended up at was the most appealing to him:

> The reason I chose it was more because I wanted to be a veterinarian and or marine biologist; right now, I'm leaning more toward marine biologist. I was looking at the other vo-tech schools, and that was the only one with biotechnology. So, I was like, "That's where I want to be." And now, for my co-op, I'm actually going to work at a veterinary clinic.... I'll be working the front desk, checking the animals and seeing what's wrong with them, and then sending them to where they need to go. So yeah, it's really fun.

Ian's school gave him both more autonomy and more hands-on experience. "You get to pick a shop you're interested in, which includes wide-ranging areas like biotechnology, and you do class blocks on that shop as sophomore and junior, and then senior year you get a job in that area for 20 hours a week, and that counts as credit."

Though there was an application process, the program was part of a public choice network where they reviewed records of attendance and behavior, rather than grades, to determine who was accepted. In other words, students didn't have to have a history of academic performance to be allowed in, as is often the case with dual-enrolled programs, but they still weren't obligated to take all students the way public schools do.[31] Programs like Ian's and Eddie's, where vo-tech classes can be part of college preparedness, and the fact that both Eddie and Ian discussed the programs they participated in as a matter-of-fact part of their education makes it clear that stigmas about vocational school being synonymous with lower quality education has started to change. So, for parents reading who haven't considered investigating what options are available locally, it's worth checking where you may have unconsciously ruled out options that could be a great fit for your teen to consider. Even the choice not to leverage a program like this, as long as it feels like a real decision and not a performative one, can help build more engagement with the more traditional approach to high school by shifting it from default to deliberate.

Caprielle: Dual enrollment via a local community college

Caprielle was one of three students we talked with who opted into a full-time dual-enrollment plan to finish out her last two years of high school:

I am technically a high school junior, but I'm doing my state dual-enrollment program, also known as Running Start, so I'm actually taking all college classes. I decided to be a full-time Running Start student rather than a part-time one, which means that I attend community college full-time. I don't step foot in my local high school. It's pretty cool. There's no part of me that regrets that decision. I made it at the end of sophomore year. My older sister did it . . . so it was nice because I really just had the path kind of laid out, and all I had to do was take the step. I didn't have to be the first one. Next year, I'm going to graduate with my Associate of Arts and Science as well as my high school diploma.

Having all of the choices was one of the things she most appreciated about Running Start. "The freedom of being able to sign up for courses. Rather than saying, 'you do English this or English that,' having the freedom to do a poetry or literature class, or expository writing, or a research paper class, it's so nice and versatile."

To Caprielle, this versatility was a sharp contrast to her high school experience before dual enrollment:

I think our education system is just so rigid and strict. It's like there's a blueprint for everything, and if you don't follow it, you're gonna fail, or you're "different." It's so typical to have your seven hours of classes, and then you have your sport or your club meeting that you go to, and then you go home and do homework, and then maybe, on weekends, you party with friends, or you just go hang out with people, or maybe you have a job. And that's the blueprint. That's every storyline you see, that's every kid that you talk to. And so, being a [dual-enrolled] student, having that freedom is really nice. I'm not studying for AP tests or anything; I'm not preparing for them because I'm not taking any of those. And having that freedom of choice for what different classes I want to take ... I have so many different options, which I'm really grateful for.

The sentiment of appreciation for a wide variety of course choices is similar to Melanie's about electives—but because all Caprielle's choices are college-level classes, and thus ones she is likely to get transferable credit for, these choices are not only meaningful but also offer a more efficient path to the college degree she ultimately wants.

However, the disadvantage of dual-enrollment programs that are done online or at a commuter college (like almost all open-access colleges are) is that these environments don't tend to lend themselves to easy connections with fellow students:

You have people of all ages here. You have moms and fathers . . . or you have other Running Start kids, or you have people fresh out of high school. It's really diverse in terms of age and race and sexual orientation, and just all labels. Though there are a lot of people, it can still be pretty hard to connect or form relationships. Especially being a Running Start student, it was intimidating being around people with so many different [experiences] when I had been so used to being in an academic environment surrounded by those my age. Though I have met a few nice students, it was through the Literature Club I founded. Running Start is really all about . . . independence and that freedom of choice and preparing for when you go to university so you can get those credits knocked out with the Gen Eds and everything. You're the one talking with your professors, always. And I am actually only doing online courses, which allows for more free time and less stress. So, it's [dual enrollment] definitely about independence and preparing ourselves rather than social dynamics, but there are, of course, opportunities.

Nina described something similar at the community college she attended—that the social opportunities don't jump out at students and how she had to go search for clubs and activities deliberately to form those connections.

For Caprielle, the difficulty of connecting was offset by having the eye-opening experiences of a diverse student body, which "put things into perspective of 'wow, everyone's life is truly different.' You truly don't understand it because you'll never experience their life." But the biggest benefit to Caprielle was in the structure:

It's just been really engaging, having a lot of freedom and free time, because I'm really getting to work on myself mentally and obviously educationally; for example, I've been applying to a lot of summer programs. So, getting to take part in those will be really nice because I won't be worrying about other things for my senior year, which people in high school probably will be worrying about.

This freedom to choose where she focused her time and energy was crucial to Caprielle and more than worth the increased challenge of connecting socially in this environment.

Connor and Zimo: Dual enrollment on a college campus away from home

Connor was also in a dual-enrollment program when we interviewed him, but he was on campus as part of the Gatton Academy, a two-year STEM program for "gifted and talented juniors and seniors."[32] The Gatton Academy is a program that allows a selected number of "high achieving" high school students (Connor noted the problems with that designation and how the tracking of students blocks many from being able to make the kind of meaningful choices about their education that he got to make) to complete their last two years of high school by taking college courses at WKU, living in a designated dorm on campus as they do so. It allows participating students both more freedom about what they learn and the chance to earn college credits for free while still in high school.

Zimo was also in a residential dual-credit program at a university. For Zimo, one of the big lessons learned was about being careful in how he exercised the greater number of choices for how to fulfill course requirements.

Zimo: So, the content is the first thing that I need to hold myself accountable for because I had the option to pick the right classes for myself, but I did not. I know very well from my experience taking AP European History that things before the Industrial

Revolution for me are quaint. That should have been the red flag, and I ignored it. Fall '21 English turned out to . . . interest me way less than I thought, and, well, it is not engaging to sit through classes talking about things you do not care the slightest bit [about].

Grace: So, you knew . . . that you didn't like that topic, but you decided to take a chance on this course?

Zimo: It's not really about taking the chance. It's more so that I didn't realize how disengaging the class would end up being and that the class happened to fit the schedule. Yes, I know that sounds pragmatic to the almost cynical extent, but that was my genuine logic.

Zimo freely admits that he used the wrong criteria to make his choice of classes, focusing on schedule rather than interest. Like Caprielle, he found out about the opportunity to do dual enrollment through family, though not quite as directly—he was talking about how boring high school was to his aunt in front of her friend, who happened to know about the program and suggested he apply. In other words, in neither of their cases were these programs well-advertised; it took hearing about them through their personal networks to realize they had options in their education, ones they were actually interested in pursuing.

Nina and King: Homeschooling can feel freeing or stifling, depending on the situation.

We spoke with two homeschooled students—one who had been homeschooled her entire K-12 education (Nina) and one who had started homeschooling right around lockdown in his final year of middle school and chose to stay there after schools opened back up (King).

In Nina's case, while she appreciated some of the freedoms homeschooling afforded her, she mostly found it uninspiring. "I taught myself French . . . I only needed a year of any language, and I ended up taking three because I was like, well, all the other subjects are done with." This kind of disinterested attitude about homeschooling pervaded Nina's descriptions of it; in contrast, she found the combination of freedom and meaningful challenge within the community that she found on campus as a college student to be far more engaging.

For King, home-schooling was a lifesaver from a school system that was grinding him down:

> *It's online, so I can take it anywhere. And the library became so much like a second home to me, not only because I was volunteering there, but it just became a family home to be able to get work that I needed. I was able to sit down and do my work when needed. And it just became kind of a second home because we've been there so often. And another thing about my learning is that [online homeschooling] gave me the opportunity to pursue things that I wouldn't have been able to pursue if I was in public school.*

These choices and opportunities energized King, especially because they stood in such stark contrast to his prior experience in public school and made him excited to learn in a way that his public school experiences had not.

Choosing Extracurriculars or Out-of-School Programs

Almost all the students we spoke to had access to extracurriculars, though not everyone participated in them. Of those who did, most shared stories of how much the right extracurricular activities really helped them feel engaged, figure out interests they didn't previously know they had, and connect with friends.

Zimo: Extracurriculars are often key to forming friendships that make school more interesting.

Zimo was one of the students who didn't participate in extracurriculars because of changes to the structure of the school day:

> *Block lunch means that everyone's dismissed at the same time, and [it] just gives us an hour or so of free time to eat lunch, do club activities, or whatever. [But] that was pretty quickly canceled after I joined them because of repeated incidents of people fighting in dining halls. I actually saw one of them. It was concerning, but without those [block lunches], they keep you in a classroom and . . . that basically means there's no way I can do things like clubs and such or make friends in general. So that makes [school] extra boring.*

The elimination of "block lunch" meant that clubs only met after school, so only students with access to private transportation could participate. Zimo had not grown up in the area, so he didn't have childhood friendships that could continue on into middle or high school. And without extracurriculars to connect with his peers, he didn't have a way to make friends as a new student.

Later, when we asked what advice he'd give to students who were trying to figure out how to improve their time in school, it was easy to see the influence of both this experience of missing out on extracurriculars and his experience of picking classes as part of his dual-enrolled program. "To the best of your range of options, tailor the classes and extracurricular activities you do to your interests." He acknowledged there can be a range of reasons students can't always do this, but still emphasized that "whenever possible, try to take classes that actually interest you instead of classes that sound fancy." Zimo also encouraged students to "facilitate change," something he wished he'd done when his school eliminated block lunch.

Connor: "We were all working together as one equal group."

Connor has stories in every section of this chapter because he focused so much on the importance of student voice and exercised his own voice in a variety of ways. One of the ways he did this was through his involvement in a state-wide student-led group called the Kentucky Student Voice Team (KSVT). He originally discovered this group when he was serving as a student advisor on his local school board. KSVT came to present to the board, and he got interested in their work and joined their online communication channel.

Several months later, around May 2020, KSVT started a project called "Coping with COVID-19," which involved surveying students from across the state and analyzing the results:

It took about 13,000 students surveyed across all of [the] Kentucky high schools. They looked at all the data for it, and they needed people to analyze it . . . to kind of sit down and work with researchers that we were pulling from the University of Kentucky, to try to really figure out how students are reacting to the pandemic and to understand things like what their home life looks like, how do they feel about their education, how do they feel about their future. Just trying to pull out these major themes that kind of got buried in the general narrative of "Oh, students are having so much learning loss; they're losing out on their math and reading skills."

Instead, this study focused on "the more social-emotional aspects of what's going on . . . more on motivation, engagement and mental health." This project was his real "starting point with the Voice Team." What was really unique about this project to Connor was that, although there were several experts involved—PhDs and postdocs from the University of Kentucky—the high school students had as much of a voice in what methods were used, and the interpretations they made from the data, as the professional researchers did. As he described it, "We were all working together as one equal group; it wasn't like the experts were the ones who made all the decisions." The simultaneous empowerment of *how* they did the project, along with the relevance of *what* they were trying to accomplish, made it a particularly meaningful extracurricular to participate in.

The shared power in this project stood in sharp contrast, in Connor's mind, to other student-voice activities he'd participated in. Connor's experience with a teacher who incorporated student interests into the design of her assignments and activities, as described in chapter two, "opened [his] eyes to the fact that I should have a say in my education." So, he started to get involved with his school system locally by becoming a student advisor to the school board, where he and other involved students "were supposed to act as a liaison between the district and the student body."

Unfortunately, this opportunity didn't lead to the kind of meaningful change he had hoped for by getting involved. "It felt very tokenizing; it felt like we weren't getting any meaningful work done, [and] it felt like we weren't affecting change or helping our communities in any way. And I didn't feel comfortable with that." Connor described several experiences when the board would ask for student input but then do nothing in response to that input. He said it felt like their reply to anything he and other students said was, "We hear you. We empathize with you. We really do care—but we're going to change absolutely nothing about what we're doing." Or, as Connor summarized it with an exasperated laugh, "I hear you and I see you; eat shit."

When he got involved with the Coping with COVID project, where "everyone in that room . . . was engaged and included," the difference was striking. With the advisory board, Connor felt like "there are words being exchanged, but . . . I can't control any of the action that's being made because of that. And that's not reported back to me in any meaningful way. I'm shouting into the void." With the KSVT project, he knew that he and his fellow high school students were full partners in "creating the project and steering it forward and doing the analysis and figuring out who does what, and why."

"Coping with COVID" was not only an empowering and exciting project to participate in, but it also caused Connor to develop additional interests that made subjects he'd previously seen as uninteresting become relevant to his longer-term goals. Whereas he had initially become interested in the Gatton Academy because he wanted to study computer science, he now started to see the opportunities it would give him to study other areas he'd previously dismissed:

I was very focused on STEM for most of my life, and the way that social sciences [are] conveyed . . . within STEM fields is like they're . . . STEM's little brother, in a sense. It's annoying, it's there, [and] we have to put up with it, but . . . we don't need to super worry about it. And so . . . being on a team and taking more of an equity lens to the world, and more of a focus on how can we actually make things better . . . despite the pandemic, despite everything that's going on, how can we as individuals on this team use our voices and . . . the stories of others to uplift and engage and change, almost radically at some times, the world that we know today. And that . . . shifted how I understood that field in general. . . . I suddenly saw the social sciences as part of myself because I knew I wanted to do good for others, and I knew those sciences were a way to do that.

This newfound interest in the power of social sciences led Connor to opt into sociology courses at WKU, which he found interesting and rewarding. He isn't the only student who shared examples of subjects feeling more relevant once applying them through engaging projects that felt more connected to their present-day life. Extracurricular programs are one potentially powerful way to have these kinds of eye-opening experiences.

Vivian: "I saw I could express myself in that sphere."

Vivian originally joined an extracurricular group just to "try something new" and because she "knew [that] for college apps, it's probably good to have a few more extracurriculars on [her] resume." Yet, it actually turned out to be incredibly meaningful. This county-wide organization, which we've anonymized as ABC to protect Vivian's privacy, provides students the opportunity to both educate themselves and even create and lead professional development for teachers in the school district:

> Early sophomore year, [I] . . . did not understand what social justice really was. . . . [But then] the more I understood the purpose behind ABC . . . and why it existed, that pushed me a little bit more to seek out other student voice clubs and other advocacy opportunities. Because that's when I started understanding why advocacy was so important, especially as a student. . . . And then, from there, it was a way for me to work toward something, but also just felt like it was morally right, in a way, because I feel like once I learned more about how society affects . . . many marginalized groups, I couldn't not do anything about it. . . . And so that became a big reason why I started seeking out more

advocacy opportunities. Because . . . those were the opportunities that I saw that I could do to help stop it. There are other ways to obviously stop and try to combat hate . . . but that was the way that I saw that I could express myself in that sphere.

The impact of ABC on Vivian wasn't just because of its focus on student advocacy and taking steps against hate and discrimination, as Vivian discovered when she sought out other extracurriculars with similar goals—*how* they did this work made a bigger difference than she expected:

Because the people in ABC are just so amazing. I am in other organizations that do promote student voice, and they are advocacy groups. But from my experience, they are not comparable to ABC because ABC, the community around it, is really warm. And the people in it are, not only are they educated . . . and the students and the staff are inspiring, but they're very welcoming to newcomers . . . who aren't very experienced in the world of advocacy. I tend to notice that there are a lot of other advocacy groups that tend to be kind of elitist. So, I think that's why I tend to gravitate toward ABC.

The focus on relationships and community reminded us of other students who also described their most engaging teachers as ones who cared about them as people, not just about their performance.

The other key part of how adults in ABC engaged with students that struck Vivian immediately was the level of autonomy and respect they afforded students:

The way the sponsors would speak to us was . . . just so nice, because I didn't feel like I was below their level, if that makes sense. The way they treated us and the way they spoke to us was . . . as if I were their equal. So, I didn't really feel that power dynamic that I tend to feel in the classroom sometimes. The

sponsors would speak to me in a way where I just really felt wel-
comed. And I wanted to come back; I was genuinely so excited
to be there every single day. And this is super minor . . . but they
would allow us to just go to the bathroom, [and] you didn't have
to raise your hand and ask, "Can I go to the bathroom?" It was
just if you got to go, just go. It's like, "You guys are teenagers,
you're almost adults, [and] you should have the power and the
ability to go and use the bathroom whenever you need to." All of
us interns, we all knew it's probably not the smartest idea to go
to the bathroom during a very important part of the lesson or
when someone was in the middle of presenting something really
important. We all knew that. So, there were never any issues
where it was like, "Hey, you shouldn't go to the bathroom." But
that made me feel so in control of my body in a way because
before, you were always taught [to ask], "Hey, can I go to the
bathroom?" And . . . you had to be back in the classroom in like
three minutes. And as a woman, sometimes, you can't do that.
You can't force yourself to be in the bathroom for only three
minutes. Especially if it's that time of the month. . . . So being in
a space where they treated us like adults, or just maybe human
beings, made me want to come back every day and want to give
more effort to the program because I was being treated really
well there.

Being treated as equals was key to a meaningful extracurricular experience for both Vivian and Connor. And like
Connor, Vivian's overall approach to school changed. Participating
in ABC, and specifically being able to co-create and deliver
professional development to teachers in her district, made
"school feel more relevant" to her because she felt like she was
doing something that made a difference, something that was
immediately and directly applicable to improving her own
high school experience and that of her peers.

Elena and Ava: Getting support from outside programs when school doesn't provide it.

As mentioned in the peer chapter, Elena went to a school that had minimal support for artists, so she needed to find regional programs to pursue her interest in art. The program she found was both deeply rigorous and "really fun because I got to choose what I wanted to do. And then, because I had that agency, I was able to engage in it with my whole heart."

For Ava, participating in organizations was crucial to offset the numbing effects of her school day, which she found dull and constricted (Ava's principal wouldn't add an option for honors courses to the school when she and her friends requested it). This was especially the case in finding support for her future goals. "There's not really a lot of future support here, I'd say that, but I get a lot of that out of the organizations I'm in versus in the school structure."

Ava's favorite organization is a national one called HOBY, a youth leadership organization with a range of programs and chapters across the U.S. HOBY exists "to inspire and develop our global community of youth and volunteers to a life dedicated to leadership, service, and innovation."[33] Ava described their international seminar as "amazing" and said, "I still talk to a lot of my HOBY friends."

One of the things Ava most appreciated about HOBY was the welcoming environment at the international seminar, which was created just by virtue of who they picked to lead the program:

It was our main speaker, and he was in charge of making sure we were all engaged, and he was amazing. I'd say he radiated personality. He was an African American who was gay. So, it was walking around with a rainbow flag and just full-out Rambo. And when you first walked in, he was what you saw. And it was just like, automatically, this is a place where I can just be myself.

Especially coming from a small town [in a Southern state], where everybody has such inside views. Nobody really looked outside. I walked in, and I was like, "This is very different from what I have in [my home state]. And I love it." I'd say a lot of people, especially the closeted people, when they walked in, everybody was like, this is a place where I can be me.

Even though Ava herself didn't identify as LGBTQ+, the obvious inclusivity for that community made her also feel welcomed.

Ava also learned from the speakers at the HOBY seminar about the ways in which gender can play a role in leadership.

Ava: They talked a lot about sexism and women in business, and, honestly, it stuck out to me that I was engaged. There was this one lady; I think she was a representative in [my home state]. And she [said] people still ask her . . . why she was working when her husband could be working too. They asked her, "Where's your daughter? Who's watching your kids?"

Grace: And why did that resonate with you?

Ava: Just because I thought we've come so far that this didn't happen. And I'd say I am kind of an activist. I'm just not very engaged in it, but that should not still be happening in this generation, where we are, where we've come so far. She's a powerful woman, . . . working in the Capitol, and somebody asked her why she worked when she's done so much.

The combination of surprise and relevance to Ava's own interests—not in being a politician, but in being a female professional—made that experience especially engaging for her.

HOBY's welcoming and relevant environment set the stage for learning and connecting in ways Ava really appreciated.

Ava: Honestly, there's a lot of speakers that I really related to, and they talked about things from a different point of view that was well needed, and I wish I would have done it sooner because I only did it my senior year. And I wish I could have had that earlier in my high school years, so I would [have been] more involved.

Grace: In your high school or in HOBY?

Ava: In my high school. In just reaching out for different programs. I'd say I don't do a lot of things outside of school just because I have very strict parents, and they don't like me going anywhere. But, for example, [a nearby university] does a summer program for juniors, and I didn't know about that. And I wish I would have done HOBY earlier because they talked a lot about doing outside programs, and I could have researched some outside programs and done them. Like this year, I'm doing a lot of outside programs this summer.

Unlike Caprielle, Ava didn't have older siblings who could make her aware of outside programs she could participate in and pave the way for parental buy-in to those programs. Additionally, the rural high school she attended didn't seem to have much information to educate students about regional and national opportunities either. So, it was entirely on her to both discover and advocate for programs that she was interested in. Ava appreciated that HOBY brought her together with people she could form lasting friendships with, put on an inspiring and thought-provoking event, made her aware of other opportunities to broaden her horizons, and ultimately deepened her sense of agency.

———————————

Melanie: "It's really therapeutic for me . . . it makes life more vibrant."

One national opportunity that Melanie said she recommends to all her friends is something called the GripTape Challenge:[34]

It's like for 14–19-year-olds. You apply for the grant, and they give you $500 to learn whatever you want. And it's super easy to get; I tell all my friends to do it, [but] for some reason, they're not doing it, I don't know. I heard about it from a friend who wanted a nice pair of ice skates. So, she said, "I'm gonna get better at ice skating," and they gave her $500 to buy a really nice pair of ice skates. I got into photography. I said, "I want to learn about wildlife photography." And they gave me $500 to get a laptop to do editing. I bought some photography equipment; I already had a camera. . . . It was super easy, super chill, and they just gave me free money, and it was great. But through that, photography has been something that I'm still doing. I did this last summer. It also looks great for college applications. Especially this year, sometimes after school, I would just go on a walk and take pictures of birds. And it's just really therapeutic for me. And to find something that you are excited about . . . it makes you more excited about life. And also, I think it just makes life more vibrant, even if it's not related to school. It's also a good way to build community with other people and find those friends that you can connect with. . . . Your life isn't just limited to your school and how well you're doing in school. . . . If you have interests, it's easier to make friends.

The program afforded her the chance to invest in an interest, and doing so didn't just improve her college applications; it made "life more vibrant" and helped her find common ground to connect with people. Though Melanie didn't discuss this aspect of the program, the Grip Tape Challenge website makes clear they also provide access to mentoring for students who receive their grants, calling to mind the benefits Zimo shared of getting access to mentors.

Ian: Founding and participating in clubs and groups

Not every student needs to go outside their immediate school environment to find meaningful extracurricular opportunities. Ian, for example, was not only able to choose a high school that had electives and internship opportunities he was interested in, but he also opted into clubs and activities—including founding an environmental club at his school, since that was an interest he had that didn't already have an extracurricular club aligned with it.

Ian, like Vivian, found that the pandemic lockdown created more space to explore other school advocacy activities. He became involved in school DEI efforts after being at a Zoom meeting during lockdown when a staff member from school talked about their goals for student involvement in this area. Ian worked closely with this staff member and other students to start affinity groups at his school. The idea to start the environmental club at his school was also sparked—though more indirectly—by another educator at the school. He had always been interested in caring for animals, and then he had a Global Studies teacher who wove conversations about environmental issues and their effect on humans and politics throughout the curriculum. That approach caused him to realize how the state of our environment impacted other aspects of the community, like:

> *food shortages in different countries and people not having homes ... It seems like every single topic you can bring up has something to do with [protecting our environment]. [So] that importance of it, combined with the fact that I already liked animals and nature, just made it really easy for me to connect to it.*

When this class ended, he founded the environmentalist club. "We've gone to the Youth Environmental Summit at [a nearby university]. We're working on starting a garden at the school; we've already got approval from the principal. And we're working on bringing recycling back." Like other students who were involved in at-school extracurriculars they liked, being involved in both the environmental and DEI groups increased Ian's interest in being at school on days he otherwise might not want to go. "I know if I have something [for one of my groups], I'm like, 'Now I really don't want to be late to school.'"

Nina: "I realized that you really have to seek out clubs and organizations."

Nina, who had been homeschooled K-12 and had worked throughout high school, had an image in her mind of what being at college would be like that didn't quite match the reality. She chose to delay her entry to college for two years after she got her high school diploma because she wanted to be clear on what she was interested in studying before she started. She said, "I knew that I wanted to ease in, and I wanted to form personal connections." She expected that opportunities to do that would be obvious, but instead found that students didn't talk much with each other before or after class or in the cafeteria (as mentioned previously, this is a common phenomenon at commuter colleges). "[I] realized that you really have to seek out clubs and organizations and things like that; it doesn't necessarily come to you. . . . I thought it would be better marketed, and it wasn't in my experience."

Once she "made that connection" that she would "have to go out and find these things," she got active in doing just that. She not only found out about the college honors program, which is described in more detail in the chapter on helpful teaching, and the writing center, which was an opportunity both to form a community and work part-time on campus, but she also got involved in "the Democratic Club" and the "Cultural Diversity Committee." She stated,

> *"What really propelled me was being taken seriously and given a voice—or given a space, like the Attic [a flexible student study and tutoring space in the college's writing center], where it's okay to make it your own, do what you want; we want you to go out and make a stand for yourself."*

In other words, the extracurriculars that were the most meaningful for Nina (and for most of the interviewees) were those that gave a structure for her to not just find people she could connect with but collaborate with them to accomplish meaningful things.

What to Do to Create Space for Meaningful Choices

As this chapter makes obvious, the easiest way for students to experience meaningful autonomy is if the adults who are in control of the surrounding structures deliberately create real opportunities for student voice and choice. And, as Connor's example makes clear, it doesn't work if this power-sharing is in name only, like it was in the school board student advisory role he played. If students don't see their opinions and perspectives being respected and valued—if they don't see real change—then it's not genuinely sharing power.

However, we're not naively claiming that power-sharing is without risks and that it's just about lifting restrictions wherever they exist. But navigating the balance between freedom and safety is a challenge that continues into adulthood: as a skill in the workplace, in raising children, or in participating in any community. Knowing there are risks to opening up real choices to young people shouldn't stop us, as adults, from pushing ourselves to make those meaningful choices available in schools—it should prompt us to involve students in helping to plan for and address those risks as part of the process of creating meaningful autonomy.

For example, at a non-profit I used to work with, we supported high-school students in identifying and building projects they cared about. In one particular case, a group of students wanted to reopen a set of bathrooms that had been closed off in their school for safety reasons. With the reduced bathroom access, the lines were long and students were invariably late for class as a result—especially female students. But the school didn't have the staff to supervise the additional bathrooms being opened up, and previously, when they had been open, students had used the unsupervised space for illicit activities like smoking. Working together, the students proposed a plan that involved students in keeping the bathrooms safe, and the school reopened them. The students who worked for the plan felt triumphant, the students who benefitted felt grateful, and the school staff realized they could have real allies in solving problems *with* the student body if only they gave them that opportunity. That kind of win is possible when adults engage teens in thoughtful collaboration—not just handing over the reins and walking away but engaging as partners to make schoolwork better for everyone.

Of course, some adults and teens may not have the energy or community necessary to make changes in their school itself, and some may not even need to. The fact that so many of the students we spoke with talked about discovering a program or organization by sheer luck or accident makes it clear just how often teens and adults don't even know about all the options that already exist to choose from. It's worth finding out about the full range of programs, partnerships, extracurriculars, and organizations that are available in your district or region that just may not be well-advertised or well-understood.

Teens and adults may not realize that they don't necessarily need to have the time or money to invest in homeschooling or private school to get more meaningful choices about how their school day unfolds. And for those who don't have any good public school-day options available and can't pursue private school or homeschool, turning to local, regional, or national extracurriculars can still make a huge difference in making it possible to learn meaningfully right now, without having to wait for high school to end.

More Ideas From Experienced Practitioners

For Parents:

- Encourage both discovery and decision-making. If you do all the research on all the options and present the best ones as a *fait accompli*, you may have found some amazing choices but still miss the mark on fostering their feelings of autonomy. At the same time, if you just wait for them to do it all on their own, apathy or overwhelm might stop them from ever finding those options that could make a difference. Look at how much independence your teen is already used to (at home and at school) and ways to take that next step further out than their current comfort zone. For instance, if they've never investigated any of the clubs and extracurriculars at their school, offer to make them a favorite meal, or add 30 minutes onto their curfew, if they come home with details about at least five groups or activities and why they would or wouldn't be interesting to try.

- Model independence and problem-solving. Let your teens see you assessing and acting on your own choices in ways to build your own sense of empowerment. Not in a performative, "look, I've got it all figured out, and I feel great every day" kind of way, but in a way that shows how you honestly wrangle with problems and find choices you didn't initially see to help you resolve them.

For Educators:

- Recognize that school rules often put pressure on teachers to treat students more like prisoners than people. Look for ways you can return students' autonomy over their bodies and time.

- Involve students in co-creating classroom activities, assignments, and norms. You'll get more buy-in if they help shape what's happening in class. But be prepared for this to take some practice if your students have never experienced anything like this before. If they don't already have a strong relationship with you, and if the school culture is generally one of student detachment and disempowerment, it will take time to build authentic student participation. Start small, once you've gotten to know them, and show them they can trust you to listen to and collaborate with them authentically.

5

How (Not) to Build Student Abilities

Learning From the Negative

"My teacher didn't really understand why I was struggling so much. She's like, 'It's not that hard.' But it is."

- Goose

"Because of how toxic he made his classroom environment . . . he just did not encourage us to ask questions."

- Elena

"Ninety percent of the time, I'm just confused [about] what I'm supposed to be searching [for] or what I'm supposed to be doing. The chemistry and math [teachers] will give us an equation or something that we can do, [something] to work with. With Global Studies, it's search this . . . and do it yourself; I'm not gonna give you any guidance."

- Avery

"I realize[d] I'm not stupid. I just don't know [the content] yet. . . . And not knowing yet doesn't mean that I'm going to get it now, or the next time, or the next time. I'll get it at some point."

- Layla

"Don't say, 'Oh, I'm not good at math.' Or 'Oh, English is my least favorite subject.' Because all those comments are putting a box

around what you can and can't do. So, I like to say this, that 'Oh, I don't know this yet.' Always put a 'yet' behind every 'I don't know.' Because that 'yet' says that where you don't know now, that does not mean that you will not know later on."

- King

Whereas the feeling of choice plays a big role in whether or not someone *wants* to learn something, the feeling of competence affects whether or not someone feels like they *can* learn something, which is why both have such a strong effect on feeling motivated about learning. Different students we spoke with felt more or less skilled in different areas. But in all cases, if a student had just one area they felt like they were reasonably good at, it served to make school more interesting (or at least more tolerable) than those for whom nothing particularly clicked.

We've already shared how, for Goose, feeling good at English made that subject one she pushed herself in academically. Ava had particular skills in math and science. Elena's love of, and skill with, art drove her to pursue programs that would continue to develop her skills. For Eddie, meeting a successful entrepreneur boosted his sense of competence as a programmer because he saw how someone who "wasn't far from where" he was at his age could "get to this level one day." And for Ian, the clubs he led further built his sense of competence, especially when he presented at a district meeting that had students from four different schools. Ian's group had the most slides and most activities, and when "even the teachers out of [our] school see what we're doing, they're like, 'Oh, aren't you doing this? Aren't you doing that?' It's nice to know that there are people who are looking and appreciate the work that's being done." Knowing that he and his peers were doing excellent work supported his confidence that he would succeed in making a difference with the environmental and DEI clubs he was active in.

However, students also discussed the barriers to their ability to learn, many of which focused on how teachers approached their students or their content, and that's the focus of this chapter. Before we launch into this theme, we want to be especially clear about our intent in sharing these stories. Yes, as in any profession in the world, there are some people who probably shouldn't be doing it and may even be doing harm to others by staying in a job they shouldn't keep. But our overall position—and one shared by the students we interviewed—is that teachers deserve more empathy than judgment. Though discussions of "de-implementation"[35] have started to surface as so many educators began leaving the position post-COVID, those discussions typically remain theoretical and hypothetical, with few practical steps taken to lift actual burdens off teachers' long daily lists of to-dos.

Parents have room to get involved here, to advocate with their school boards about what to take *off* teachers' plates so that only the most important things are left on them. These stories are meant to spark ideas of why it's important to make sure the standards teachers are held to are the ones that actually catalyze students' ability to learn and to give adults material to share with the young people they care about that might help those students feel less alone. By opening up a space for dialogue about how to approach (or avoid) learning environments that make students feel incapable of succeeding, we can help students see how a bad classroom experience is simply that and not an indication of whether they can build and find interest in a particular academic skill.

Building Abilities Requires Structure and Support

Frequently, when asked to describe their least engaging learning experiences, interviewees spoke about just not having enough structure or support to know how to succeed in the class. Without that support and structure, students struggle to know what abilities they need to build and how to build them.

Goose, Maria, and Avery: We need clarity and consistency.

For example, Goose described the effects of receiving inconsistent feedback from a psychology teacher who "didn't really make [her] feel good throughout the entire year":

> *She did try; it was just that I was struggling, and then she did other things throughout the year that made me feel like, "Oh, you don't really care." But she would say things like, "Oh, you're doing so much better. I'm so proud of you." And so sometimes, like when it's obvious that you're putting the effort in, and they tell you that they're proud of you, that does make the difference. But . . . if you have an already kind of bad experience with a teacher, and they're suddenly saying, "Oh, I'm so proud of you," [you wonder], "Are you going to be proud of me in a month?"*

This is akin to the training that managers sometimes receive on how to make sure they actually support their employees' success rather than simply act supportive. There's a difference between providing the structures, clarity, and scaffolding people need to actually know what expectations are and meet them versus providing emotionally supportive and sympathetic comments that don't change anything about the reality of a working or learning environment (other than making the manager seem like a nice person). As both a manager and a teacher, it's easy to end up just being "supportive" without actually providing the needed *support* for real success.

Maria talked about something similar when she was contrasting her experience in two Spanish classes that she had over two years. The first one was confusing, in part because it happened during COVID and "it was online, and we were having internet issues, and it was a mess," and in part because of how the teacher taught, with only spoken instructions and unclear expectations. In contrast, the following year was "more enjoyable [because] . . . we have more content, we have rubrics, she is with us, and she explains it in a way we can understand." All of those things added up to actual support that translated to student success.

And Avery talked about how essential clarity is to make good use of work time during class. This came up in response to his descriptions of his engaging math and science teachers, which were shared previously. We wondered if part of what was making those classes engaging was being provided time to work independently during class, with the teacher circulating to help, and Avery said that, unlike with math and science, he didn't like having open work time in his global studies and English classes:

> *Ninety percent of the time, I'm just confused [on] what I'm supposed to be searching [for] or what I'm supposed to be doing. The chemistry and math [teachers] will give us, like, an equation or something that we can do, [something] to work with. With Global Studies, it's 'Search this . . . and do it yourself, I'm not gonna give you any guidance.' So, it's a lot more challenging. But it's not that I don't enjoy a challenge, it's just, I don't know how to put it, it's just not engaging at all, it makes me not want to do it when I have to search something up and I can't just do it from my memory.*

Part of the difference in what creates a sense of clarity relates to the field. In the humanities, the key skills under development are typically related to conducting, interpreting, and writing about things you read. In STEM, the key skills under development are typically focused on remembering key natural laws and principles and applying them, whether to an equation or an experiment. If one of these skill sets is easier for a student than another, then it will take a lot more support to create clarity in the less comfortable skill set.

Avery struggled a bit when trying to describe what the difference between these two different approaches, STEM vs the humanities, is like for him:

Everything math and chemistry, as you're doing it, just clicks into place, and it gives you that little reward sensation whenever you get a question right. For other things, it's not that it doesn't, but it's just, I don't know, I just hate doing stuff like that. I really don't know how to explain it.

Of course, those who struggle with math and chemistry would disagree that, for them, everything "just clicks into place" as they're doing it, but for Avery, it was very easy to describe what chemistry and math felt like to do, and how the sense of transparency meant he could feel accomplished and rewarded by work time.

In contrast, even trying to describe why the work for other classes didn't feel that way left him groping for the right words—even what the lack of clarity felt like was itself unclear. So, we asked what happened when he hit moments like that:

I'm thinking, "Maybe I can put this off 'til later; I really want to go on my phone right now, [and] I just, I don't want to do this. I want to speak to my friends; I want to—" [There's] just so many other things I feel like I can do because, when I finish a big assignment for English or Global Studies or whatever it is, it just doesn't give me that reward sensation that I get from finishing a single math problem. That takes five minutes compared to a month-long assignment or weeklong assignment. Another thing is that, as opposed to [feeling] like a reward, it just feels like this stress off my shoulders, but then I know that I'm going to get assigned another thing two weeks later.

For Avery, the feeling that there were "so many more things I can do" than succeed in these more humanities-oriented classes meant he felt less willing to work on them, less able to stay on task when given work time, and less accomplished when the work was completed.

On top of all of this, he felt like the teacher was just perpetually judging them for not meeting expectations without giving them the structure or support they needed in order to understand and meet those expectations.

Avery: My English teacher has said multiple times throughout the semester [that] . . . if we can't do this assignment, we shouldn't be in her class. It's unnecessary and just makes me feel like, you know, I have to get a really good grade on this. But, at the same time, I just don't like that type of teaching.

Becca: What's the context, usually, when she says stuff like that?

Avery: It's not that students aren't listening. It's like she'll go on for 30 minutes explaining the assignment, wasting the entire class, which eventually gets boring. So, they stop paying attention. And then she'll say, . . . "If you can't do this, you shouldn't be in my class; you should get out."

This dynamic illustrates one of the big problems that arise from the fact that there are such different mental skills and habits needed to succeed in STEM vs humanities subjects. Teachers usually don't become teachers of subjects they struggled with and disliked, so they're unlikely to immediately understand and relate to the needs of students who find the fundamental skills of their subject area alien and confusing. In other words, the English teacher has every reason to feel like she explained everything in great clarity because she likely explained it in a way that would have worked perfectly for her when she was a student. It's much harder to explain things in a way that works for a brain that processes information very differently than your own.

I experienced the difficulty of spotting this from the educator's side. When I was a new writing professor, and I was struggling to understand why some of my students just didn't seem to get seemingly basic things about writing, no matter how often I talked about them, my advisor explained this to me as the difference between "implicit" and "explicit" learners. She came from a family of engineers and said she would have been one herself if she hadn't been born at a time and place where women going into engineering just wasn't a thing, where the assumption was that if she was going to go into an academic field, it would have to be English. But her brain worked more like an engineer's brain, and she worked hard to make all the implicit expectations of writing become explicit so she could learn it. Later, this meant she was very effective at teaching it to students who found writing more confusing than science and math.

If I hadn't worked closely with her, I may not have ever realized how many of my expectations for what good writing looked like were tacitly woven into my beliefs of what it meant to be a good student who was capable of, and interested in, success. After all, effort had always been the main variable that made a difference in how well I did in class, so if my students weren't succeeding, I unconsciously assumed it was because they either weren't putting in the effort or just weren't capable of developing the skill. And as a parent, I'm especially grateful for my advisor because my older son is far more like Avery than he is like me—so it has helped tremendously for me to be able to help him see the implicit expectations of good writing and good research. It hasn't caused him to enjoy those subjects (much to my sadness since I love writing), but it has at least helped him avoid the belief that he is just a "bad writer" who will never be capable of succeeding in that area of schoolwork.

Melanie: "Her tests were unreasonable because she would put information on the test that she just didn't teach us."

Though Melanie had experienced excellent support in some of her most challenging chemistry and math classes, she also had her least supportive experience in one specific chemistry class—in her case, AP chemistry in her high school:

> *This year, I think my two hardest classes were my calc class and my chem class. Calc: my teacher is excellent. She's very intensive, I've never had so much homework from a teacher, but she is excellent. She's there for help. She's responsive. She knows what she's doing. My [AP] chem teacher, I think the class is easier than calc, but . . . I'm just trying to get through; I'm just trying to get that grade up so it's not a red flag to colleges.*

This orientation to just "get through" just enough for a grade caught us by surprise. She was not only one of the highest academic performers we interviewed, but she was also genuinely interested in learning.

After further questioning, it turned out that there were a couple of superficial similarities between the AP math and AP chemistry teachers. For instance, both gave a difficult test in the first week of class, based on summer work, that most students failed. Like they did in AP calculus, Melanie and her classmates both panicked about what failing that initial test meant for the rest of the school year. Unlike the response when they came to talk to the AP calculus teacher, however, the AP chemistry teacher dismissed their concerns. Melanie explained, "We tried to talk to her, like, 'Can we raise our grades? Can we do corrections? Can we do something?' . . . Our grades were in the C's, and we're like, 'We're trying to get into college; this is a red flag for college.'" But the teacher's response was just "It'll be fine." So, Melanie and her classmates went to school administrators, but the teacher "was unresponsive [and] mad that we were going over her head to administration." In fact, "when another student, who wasn't in our class, was talking to her, she was like, 'Oh, I hear they're going to administration . . . they do that every year, . . . but I have tough skin, it doesn't get to me.'" To Melanie, hearing that was a flag that "there's an issue here; there's a disconnect" when a teacher who got repeated complaints from students year after year viewed it as a matter of just needing to have tough skin, rather than an indication she might need to shift something about her teaching to support students feeling able to succeed.

This impression of disinterest in student voice was furthered by noticing that when "a couple of really smart kids in my class . . . would correct her" incorrect chemistry information, "she would be very unresponsive to that. . . . And it was just so stressful because all of us are AP kids trying to get into college." Surprisingly, Melanie described the teacher as "one of the nicest people I know" and said, "She got better after . . . we all kind of calmed down. And she's fine now that we're all done with testing, and she's very nice." But this kind of belated niceness was irrelevant to Melanie and her classmates because it didn't translate to helping them with what was actually important to them: knowing how to successfully learn the relevant material prior to being tested on it.

Instead, they approached the class with a "just get the grade up" attitude because they felt like that was the only option that was in their control. Melanie explained:

If her grades and her tests are going to be unreasonable, it's a waste of my time to study for them anyway. Her tests were unreasonable because she would put information on the test that she just didn't teach us. And then there would be no curve;

there'd be no nothing. So, it's just like, "It's a waste of my time. I'll just accept that. That's going to be the grade that's going to be low. I'll explain about it on my college app."

In this story, it's not too hard to have empathy both for Melanie and for her teacher. Teachers perennially get frustrated with students who seem only focused on getting their grades up rather than on learning, and we could imagine why a teacher might want to start students with failing tests in the first week to try to get their attention that they'll need to push themselves hard if they want to succeed. Similarly, the stress that the students feel in these classes is also very real. It's a natural byproduct of encouraging students to pursue the best college education they can get, which prompts students to fixate on how certain extracurriculars and grades will look on a college application. This can put students and teachers at odds with each other when a teacher is focused on making class content rigorous and is not willing or able to provide extra support, like Melanie's math teacher did, to support students excelling at that level of rigor.

Layla: It "was the least I've ever learned . . . she allowed you to do whatever you wanted."

Layla described a very different kind of missing support for her senior year Spanish class. He explained:

It was the least I've ever learned in a classroom. She allowed you to do whatever you wanted in that class—no classwork, [you could] sit and talk with friends, leave and come back—whatever you wanted as long as you handed the assignments in. Even if it was late, she allowed full makeup work with no deductions [for] the entire year, even if you handed it in on the last day of school.

Safe to say I got a good grade, but I don't know a lick of Spanish.

Other chapters address the importance of students feeling like they have meaningful choices in what and how they're learning because it's almost impossible to sustain any motivation for that learning without it. However, autonomy without any feeling of relevance also makes learning unlikely. It's worth noting that the flexible deadlines aren't actually the problem in this example; Layla had a chemistry teacher she learned a lot from who also allowed assignments to be turned in late without deductions. But that teacher allowed late work because she was pushing students to actually master each foundational concept before moving to the next, whereas Layla's description of the Spanish class makes it clear she wasn't required to demonstrate actual proficiency with Spanish to move through the class.

It's Hard to Learn When You Feel Dismissed or Unsafe

In direct contrast to the stories of kind teachers who care about their students' success and lives in general, almost every student has experiences with teachers or staff members whose behavior falls somewhere on a spectrum from dismissive to outright cruel. Unfortunately, this seems as inevitable in education as it is in work life, to encounter someone with power over you who does not wield that power well—but unlike in the workplace, where employees can at least try to find a new boss, students are generally stuck with who they've got. Feeling stuck and without meaningful choices is demotivating enough—feeling that way around an adult who seems anywhere from unsympathetic to outright mean causes students to feel incapable of learning in those environments, and so they generally give up.

Goose, Ian, and Grace: "You should know that already."

It really undermines students' confidence in their abilities when teachers seem baffled that students find something hard to do. Goose, for example, contrasted the encouragement she received from her English teacher, a class she felt capable in, with a math teacher she'd gone to with questions. "My teacher didn't really understand why I was struggling so much. She's like, 'It's not that hard.' But it is."

Ian shared a similar example of one teacher, whom we'll call Ms. N, who stood in stark contrast to most of the teachers in his vo-tech school. When he would greet her at the start of class by saying "Good morning" as she walked in, she would say "Hi, Ian" but "in a tone like 'Oh, it's you.'" When the whole class was talking and didn't quiet down quickly enough, she singled out Ian to come sit up in the front corner, where he couldn't see the smart board with that day's lesson content on it. He pointed this out, and she said, "Well, you should have thought of that," and so he effectively missed that day's lesson.

This continued throughout the year: when he or other students asked her for help, Ms. N would say things like, "We went over this, so you need to do it yourself." He added:

> It wasn't even [just] me who was struggling in her class; a good portion of the people in that class, almost pretty much everyone, even the people that had really good grades, [were struggling to understand]. That was probably their hardest class, which I'm pretty sure is because she wasn't the most enthusiastic teacher. If I'd ask for help, she'd be like, 'You should know that already.' And I'm like, 'Well, we don't, and it's kind of your job to teach us. So, I don't know what you want me to do at that point.'

There was a second teacher in the class "who was the complete opposite" and whom all the students "loved." This teacher, if Ian or others asked for help, "was glad to help." And Ian suspected this teacher was "aware of the way [Ms. N] acted" and was trying to offset the negative effects because the second teacher "would always try to cut in when [Ms. N] would try to have some type of attitude ... to boost our spirit a little bit."

This could happen across any subject, any time an educator fails to notice their assumptions about the diversity of what effort and talent can look like. For example, when Grace was taking her Organic Chemistry course:

> *I didn't quite understand how to articulate my needs and expectations for my professor when I needed help. I would struggle with wording my questions, unsure how to explain what was confusing me. Often, he would answer a different one, assuming he understood what I was asking without probing first for the root of my confusion. Eventually, I noticed he was less likely to call on me and other students in the course who asked fuzzy questions, instead seeming to favor those students whose questions were more succinct and clear. Sometimes, I got the impression that he had conflated the ability to ask clear questions about organic chemistry with an interest in learning organic chemistry. Maybe he assumed that those of us who asked weaker questions did so out of lack of interest and effort. I didn't even realize how much of an effect his approach had on my sense that I could learn difficult material until I had another professor who would ask questions about our questions. She made sure she understood why we were confused before she framed her answers, and it made a huge difference for me and other students in her class.*

Grace described how she left that class feeling like she was "understood and seen" by her professor. As a result, she "felt ready to tackle hard concepts and master difficult skills," both in that course and subsequent courses.

Any parent who has felt like they have repeated explanations to their kids dozens of times may not find it too hard to have empathy for Goose's math teacher, Ian's Ms. N, or Grace's chemistry professor. But that same empathy can allow us to understand how an overall feeling of burnout, of being continuously ignored, could easily cause educators to assume a student wasn't paying attention[36] when, actually, that student was genuinely finding a topic difficult to wrap their minds around. And if teachers think they're explaining, but they're actually just repeating themselves—like Avery's math teacher who answered a request for clarification by repeating the exact same explanation three times—it's easy to imagine how this can become a vicious cycle where teachers and students both feel dismissed or ignored by each other, and both become convinced that certain students simply aren't capable of learning.

Elena: Mocking students makes class "confusing" and "toxic."

Elena had an AP calculus teacher in her senior year who would "berate students in an immature manner." For example, the tradition for seniors in her school was to skip school on the day of prom to spend time getting ready, and the day before, the teacher jeered, "How many of you are too ugly to have to skip school tomorrow to get ready for prom?" Elena said the class went silent, "just waiting for him to say, 'Oh, that was a bad joke,' but, well, he never said that."

She said he extended this mockery to their math acumen as well. He typically would call on specific students to answer questions, and if they didn't understand or didn't get it right, he would make fun of them. Elena said this happened to her periodically because she frequently didn't understand his lessons. But he also would pick on students who got things right:

So, Steven was actually quite good at math. [But] for some rea-

son, this teacher didn't like him. So, he would just say, "Oh, Steven, you're too smart for your own good. Do you think that you can teach better than me?" Or he would go on a rant like that. And so, it'd be very uncomfortable.

To Elena and other students, there was no way to make this teacher happy—get things right or wrong, and it didn't matter; he was still going to mock your abilities.

This disposition extended even to his test-grading practices, which puzzled us so much we had to ask Elena to describe it twice. We were, apparently, just the most recent of many who needed to ask a lot of questions to understand his grading process:

You know how an X looks like it's like two lines? So, whenever he graded our answers, if they were correct, he would put half an X in red. So, it was very confusing for us . . . whenever we got our graded assessments back. . . . It would always feel a little bit startling because we would see the half X's, and it would look like everything on the paper was wrong because everything was in red or everything looked like they could be part of an X . . . It obviously wasn't normal to grade like that. But because of how toxic he made his classroom environment . . . he just did not encourage us to ask questions. And so, after we got our first graded assignment back . . . we had to wait a long time before I was like, "I guess nobody else is going to ask."

So, Elena finally raised her hand and asked, "How do we know which one is correct and which one is incorrect?" The teacher looked like "he wanted to be snarky, but then he noticed other students looking at him, so he was like, 'Oh, the half X is correct. And then a whole X is incorrect.'" In other words, rather than leaving correct answers blank and only marking their incorrect ones or marking correct ones with a different shape or color than the incorrect ones, this teacher was so interested in saving time that he started each answer assuming he might as well start marking it wrong—and then, if they turned out to be right, leave the mark there and proceed to the next one. While this might be an efficient way to see at a glance how many questions you've graded in case you get interrupted while grading, the effect on students, especially when combined with the rest of the classroom environment, was both "confusing" and "toxic," undermining any sense of competence that they had around math even when they got things right.

Unsurprisingly, his class was the most disengaging one Elena had ever encountered in her entire K-12 experience:

> It just felt like a waste of time and that we were just sitting there because we were supposed to fulfill a calculus requirement, but we weren't allowed to do it in a study hall manner. Like, if I had my way, I would have rather just watched math YouTube videos because I would have been more productive. But instead, we had to be in the presence of this man who had his own anger management issues and who took out his issues . . . onto his students for like 80 minutes every day. . . . I would actually say I was grateful for masks . . . [because] at the beginning of the school year, it was a little bit easier to conceal my emotions behind my medical mask, at least, because whenever he pulled those things like that, I feel like I didn't give him as much power over me because he couldn't really tell what I was thinking.

It was so bad that Elena and a few other students tried to "lobby the senior counselor to change [their] schedule to a lower-level math," but they were unsuccessful. As a result, they spent the rest of the year just trying to ignore him as best they could and do well enough to keep their grades from interfering with their ability to graduate.

Tuesday: "I definitely wish that they would understand more about the mental health struggle."

Like King, Tuesday, also experienced a school and peer environment that did not welcome him. At the time of interviewing him, Tuesday was all set to finish high school and go to college to study biology and minor in Chinese literature. However, to get to that point, he had to overcome significant barriers from people around him. His peers alternately ostracized and harassed him, and the teachers and staff in his school, as well as his parents, did nothing to stop it. All of this meant his ability to learn and succeed in his classes ultimately took a back seat to building the abilities and skills to navigate stress, rejection, and danger.

Being both biracial and trans made him more vulnerable to ridicule and exclusion in his hometown. In middle school, it was common for Tuesday to be called "Panda" by other kids, who were simultaneously making fun of his weight and his racial background:

> I used to go to school just to get my education, and then I'd want to go home. But then I'd have to worry about, "Oh, what's going to happen once I get into the halls." I'd have to worry about getting bullied when I [wanted] to do something educational. And so, it was kind of just like this background fear.

Tuesday experienced an extra layer of worry on top of the standard test anxiety many students get, one based on needing to think about what students he was going to be around each hour of class. He described the anxiety prompted by remembering things like "Oh, I also have somebody who bullies me next hour" or worrying, "What's going to happen in the hallways?"

This background of constant worry eventually began to

affect his ability to pay attention in class. He described the effect:

The way that [it] made learning harder is just because it would be one other thing that I'd be stressing out about. So, I'd be stressing out about the social aspect of school while I'm taking a test, and so sometimes I wouldn't get to the end of the test because somebody might be sitting next to me [and] they might be making a little bit of fun of me for doing something. Or just my anxiety would get to me, and they'd be looking at me, and I feel like, "Oh, they're looking at me because I got in a fight, and they're silently in their head making fun of me." Granted, some of it's probably my own fault just because I have a little bit of paranoia.

That paranoia arose from the persistent bullying and ridicule he had experienced for years. He was always on edge, scared of who might be next to hurt him, and that turned into a general social anxiety, occupying the mental space necessary for learning. All of this made going to school and wanting to learn more difficult.

The effects, for Tuesday, weren't only visible in incomplete tests and lower grades. It also affected his overall well-being:

It also made my mental health harder. And so, with that, I had to be hospitalized a few times because it just kind of made my depression and other aspects worse. It made it so that I did not want to go to school. It made me feel [I was] in an unsafe environment because nobody seemed to be advocating for [me]. I've always been a big self-advocate. But it's kind of hard to self-advocate when no one's willing to listen or help you further your advocacy. And so, I would advocate to these people like, "Hey, this is happening. Can you help me?" And they're like, "Okay, we'll try." But they don't try. So, it made it hard and made me not want to go to school.

The fact that reporting the bullying never resulted in real support from school adults and never changed anything about what happened in school prompted Tuesday to stop reporting it. Instead, he tried to deal with it on his own, though this created new problems for him.

For instance, Tuesday recalled one morning when he and another student started arguing in the parking lot outside school about politics:

I walked away eventually. And then he said something like, "Oh, if you weren't a girl, I could kick your ass." And so, then I called him back, and I'm like, "No, I'm not a girl. I'm a guy. If you're gonna do it, then do it. Don't go back on your word." So, we just kept having a little bit of an argument about that. He started calling me the D-word. And then some other words, like the F-word, and then some other trans-related slurs. And so eventually, we got into a physical altercation that had to be broken up, and the school decided to give us both three days of suspension, but other than that, nothing happened.

Then, as Tuesday put it, "the principal got on my case. He's like, 'Well, you should have just reported it instead of getting into an altercation.'" To Tuesday, this was an absurd request since he had seen how nothing happened when he had reported bullying in the past, and since he saw that the student who attacked him got no additional consequences for using anti-LGBTQ slurs against him besides the same suspension Tuesday himself got.

Tuesday did have some support in navigating these peer dynamics from one of his teachers, who encouraged him not to pay attention to verbal bullying from other students. Tuesday found it helpful when he "would have a lot of anger issues and people would get on [his] nerves" that this one teacher would remind him "not every war is [your] war. And [you] don't need to fight every fight. Because no matter what people say, at the end of the day, it's not going to matter." Tuesday also tried to distinguish between which "fights" he wanted to take on versus which ones were better to ignore:

If I know that this person is just acting out of pure ignorance because they simply don't know better, then I am willing to talk to them about what they are saying and why it's wrong. But if it's somebody that is doing it because they know it's bad, and . . . they're not willing to change, [then those are the ones to ignore]. Granted, I realize it's going to be harder to do that because I could be on the subway and somebody could say something that's [wrong]. Well, do I try to educate them and say, "Hey, maybe you shouldn't do that" or "That's wrong"? Or do I just go about and ignore it? And I've come to realize sometimes it is better just to ignore it because there's probably other people in their lives that are telling them that what they do is wrong.

For Tuesday, these kinds of reflections helped him distance himself from painful moments in school, and they evolved from strategies he learned through therapy.

However, these strategies were hard-won, imperfect, and only barely helped him enough to graduate on time amidst the significant barriers his school culture created to his learning. On top of the lack of acceptance for his gender, race, and body type, he also found that the adults around him were unsympathetic to the resulting mental health challenges he experienced from the persistent fear and lack of belonging these experiences brought on. He discussed this when we asked what he wished adults understood about his generation:

I definitely wish that they would understand more about the mental health struggle. . . . I had to go inpatient two weeks ago just because a lot of things were getting really bad, and so I just knew that I had to be impatient for a bit. And then, when I got out, I had to start catching up with schoolwork. But none of my teachers were really [supportive]; they all knew what was happening, but they still would not give me leeway when I was trying to turn work in. . . . And it was also because, the last Friday [before graduation], I had to turn everything in for graduation, all my assignments. And so, I talked to the principal. I was like, "I can get this done on Saturday." He's like, "No, you have to get it done now, or you won't be walking." And so, I had to . . . do over two weeks of homework for two different classes just so that I'd be able to graduate, and they gave me no leeway on it whatsoever. Which, to me, made no sense . . . [because] my freshman year . . . I went inpatient twice for my freshman year. I was getting pretty badly bullied then . . . that's when I also socially came out . . . that's the first time I ever went inpatient. And so, afterwards, I had a few essays and some other things in my English class. And so eventually I got them done, but when it came to my senior year and I asked for an extension, the teacher said, "You can't have an extension. You have been awful with turning your things in on time." But I haven't been; I've always turned my things in on time unless there was something big like a hospitalization or an inpatient. So, it made no sense, and I tried to point that out, but the teacher just went on with it.

When we asked what happened next, Tuesday said, "I just smiled and nodded and kept going on with the class because I really liked that class and I really liked that teacher. I just felt . . . that it was a little rude of her to say such a thing because I'd been a pretty diligent student of hers." Tuesday also said, "I understood her perspective that I should have maybe talked a little bit more about it."

Tuesday managed to graduate on time. However, we can't help but wonder whether the same reaction would have happened if Tuesday had been an inpatient in the hospital for a physical ailment. There may have been legitimate local or state laws that were immovable, regardless of circumstances, and a student who had been inpatient due to a physical ailment might have been told the same thing. But that wasn't how it was explained to Tuesday, and maybe if it had been, it would have felt more like getting support in confronting a difficult challenge rather than putting extra hurdles in his way based on a seeming belief that he was just "awful with turning things in on time." When treatment from peers and adults makes it both psychologically and physically unsafe to be who you are and adults do nothing to stop it, maintaining a belief in your ability to learn becomes even harder, and it requires additional resources both to address those additional barriers to learning and to protect students from lasting harm.[37]

Content Matters

While teachers can choose to talk to their students in respectful rather than dismissive ways and can choose what kind of structures and supports they offer around their assignments, they usually *can't* choose their curriculum—the pacing, the learning objectives, the materials, and so on. Increasingly, they sometimes can't even choose *how they talk about* that preselected curriculum without coming under scrutiny from an administrator concerned about angry parents[38] or politicians looking for a soapbox to jump on. Ariya alluded to the dampening effect this can have when she talked about how she imagined her most engaging classroom experience, a challenging discussion of the murder of Emmett Till, would have been received in the political climate around education in 2022: she suspected the teacher would have been reprimanded, or at least told to select new content, and that everyone's learning would have suffered as a result.

Sometimes, making classroom content meaningful requires

change to happen at the level of state and city policy and culture rather than at the level of the individual classroom or school building. To understand why that kind of advocacy is worthwhile, it helps to hear exactly how irrelevant, inaccurate, or unstimulating content affects students' ability to learn.

Ava: "It's like you're just here to do the work and go on; you're not here to learn."

For Ava, disengaging content had to do with the fact that her teacher, from her perspective, held the whole class back:

> *If it's something I already know or can easily look at the problem and learn, I don't like to engage in class. Just because, when paying attention in class, and she's going through the stuff I already know, I've done a lot, and then, because some people don't get it as fast as me, she has to slow down even more, so then at the end of every class we have a homework assignment, so usually I just do the assignments while she's teaching, so then after she's done and I'm done, I help other people. I think in this class, the teacher is incredibly smart, but she is so smart it's so hard for other people to learn it, so then, to learn it, she has to really dumb it down.*

To a student struggling to get it, this might have looked like support (or maybe it would have looked like Avery's English teacher, explaining something for 30 minutes while everyone tuned out). For Ava, it meant being too bored to stick with the pace of the class.

Like this situation does for many teachers, it also caused Ava to wonder how many of the students were actually struggling and how many just didn't care.

> *Ava: The work is so easy that anybody should be able to pass. Even if it's with a bad grade, with a D, like some of the electives*

classes are just incredibly easy. . . . We'd start off the week doing terms, and then do a study guide, and then take the test, and the test is exactly what's on the study guide. And people still managed to fail that. . . . And that just makes me realize that nobody really cares.

Grace: So, no one really cares about learning?

Ava: Yes. And I feel like school is not really a place of learning, especially not here. My old [high school] principal, he moved last year, [but] we wanted advanced classes. And he told us straight out that he does not want to cater to the few students who could be doing better. . . . He just wanted [us] to excel in the classes we were already in.

Grace: So, it seems to me that the collective understanding is that students just don't care about their classes, about what they're learning, because it's not really stimulating—like they're not doing anything different?

Ava: It's more like you're just here to do the work and go on; you're not here to learn the work, if that makes sense.

Grace: Kind of. Can you unpack that for me?

Ava: [It's] like . . . you're coming to school to do a worksheet, like [for example] a reading worksheet, and all of the answers are in the texts. It's like coming to school to do one of those worksheets every day and just going back home.

Having boring content alongside low expectations made for a very disengaging learning environment for Ava and led her to feel frustrated by her peers, teachers, and school administrators.

When we asked her what one thing she wished adults would do better, she said she wished adults would productively push students toward success:

There's not a lot of encouragement going. Like, if there are students doing bad [sic], they're like, "Oh, that's all you can do.

That's fine." There's no "you should do better" [or] "you should strive to be your best." . . . [Students here] don't know how [school will affect them. They think that if they don't do well that nothing happens—and that's true, if you do badly [here], nothing happens, but they don't know what happens if you do really good, like all the scholarships you [could] get, or is it connection, opportunities—they don't know about that.

Though Ava used the word "encourage," she isn't necessarily referring to the kind of soft and squishy, kind words about effort that people might associate with that word. Instead, she means encouraging students to succeed by making the stakes relevant and giving content that matches those stakes—a far more active role than just being encouraging.

Some readers might notice a tension between Ava's story here and the stories from Avery and Grace about teachers who didn't convey content in a way that worked for all their students. Facilitating a class so that it is a meaningful challenge to all the students in it, regardless of their pre-existing knowledge and confidence in the subject, is one of the hardest parts of a teacher's job (and it's a job filled with hard parts). We imagine her teacher was grateful that Ava would turn to help her peers once she finished her own work since that's a strategy that can be very helpful in differentiating instruction but is dependent on having students who are willing to do it. Other strategies are discussed further at the end of this chapter.

Vivian and Goose: "I constantly felt I was in that class to pass the exam, not to learn."

Of course, sometimes, certain kinds of stakes can make learning less relevant, at least for some students. This was the case for Vivian with her AP classes, where the driving focus of the class is on doing well in order to get a high score on an AP exam. For some students, this is motivating. But for Vivian, it made the classes really uninspiring:

> *Because I feel that I am in the class not to learn but to pass an exam . . . it makes me dread . . . class because so much of what we do in the class is to prepare for the exam. . . . And that's what teachers who teach AP classes should be doing, right? Teachers who teach AP classes should be teaching their students how to apply the content to the exam, and they should have worksheets and assignments to help you to prepare for the exam. But they do that because of the way AP works. And I really don't like it because I always felt like I'm not even learning. . . . I'm just learning how to take this exam. All of that time that I'm trying to learn new ways that I have to write an essay or new ways to read a multiple-choice question, I could be actually learning about, you know, American history or how government works. Because interestingly enough, while I can tell you how to write an AP [Government] FRQ [Free Response Question], I can't tell you how my county politics works. I can't tell you how the county council works and what the connection is to the Board of Education. I know now because I've had to seek that information out on my own. But as a freshman, I could tell you how to write an FRQ [for AP Government], but I had no idea how city or local politics or government worked. And I feel like that's a huge issue. Because I spent so much time learning how to read a multiple-choice question and things that are so specific to test-taking that I feel like that kind of eclipsed other important content that we could have been learning about.*

In other words, test-taking skills seemed to overshadow the actual content. We asked her how much of the time in her AP classes she would estimate was specific to test taking, and she said it seemed like it was about 30% of class time.

Vivian then clarified her opinion about her AP teachers and their choice to spend this much time on test preparation:

I just want to be clear: I don't begrudge any of my teachers for allocating that much time toward the test because it's necessary. If you want to learn how to take the exam, well, you have to put in a lot of time to learn how to take the exam: how to read the questions, the very specific way that they want you to answer things, the structure, how you want your essays to be, even though that's not how you write your essays in English class. As a teacher, you need to do that for your AP students. But I'm just saying in AP, in general, the fact that they cause teachers to do that if the teachers want their students to succeed, it's really discouraging to me because I constantly felt I was in that class to pass the exam, not to learn U.S. history.

Furthermore, it seemed clear to us that while she acknowledged that these test-taking skills were important, they were only important in the context of AP courses, as opposed to general, more versatile skills that she could apply to other courses or even future college courses.

As a direct consequence of interacting with these larger structures played out in individual AP teachers' decisions, Vivian ended up taking fewer AP courses, even though it meant getting less college credit; she wanted to prioritize learning content she cared about over learning test-taking skills and had to ignore standard advice on how to be a successful student in order to do it. Goose expressed a related feeling about her AP Psychology class for her senior year:

Why waste so much time doing grueling work for something that may not actually have been worth it in the end? Like, I really regret taking AP Psych this year because it didn't really help my grades. I thought that the class was going to be different. I didn't know it was going to be vocabulary-based. And some-

thing my teacher said was that if you memorize all six hundred words, you would get a five on the exam. And I realized, "Wow, this is not the class for me," but it was too late for me to switch out at that point.

We share these stories as a way to be aware of what AP classes can be like, not to dismiss having AP classes as an option—having more advanced class options was something Ava, for example, really wanted and was very disappointed her school didn't provide. It's the element of conscious choice that is crucial here. If it's to help with college acceptance or a credits-related goal, then AP class options are likely to be more meaningful than if, like Goose and Vivian expected, a student picks the AP class hoping it's going to be more interesting and productively challenging for learning. For both Vivian and Goose, in different states and different subject areas, they found that their AP classes were far more about doing well on the test than about meaningful learning, and that didn't line up with what they wanted to experience in the classroom.

King and Ariya: "They purposefully weren't giving us the whole truth."

Vivian was not the only student who felt like she had to go outside traditional school structures to actually get the most from their learning. Both King and Ariya sought opportunities outside of the traditional school structures in order to feel validated in their learning. King, for instance, described his frustration with the content that was covered by his public school curriculum versus what was left out:

When it comes to Black excellence and African American culture, it's scarcely been taught. When it comes to talking about ancient kingdoms, only Egypt is mentioned. . . . And I remember when I was in my seventh-grade history class, Black kingdoms were coincidentally put as the last thing, like the last unit, the last two months of school, and everyone knows that if a unit is placed at the last two months of school, then [there is] going to be absolutely little [learning] . . . because everyone's mindset is getting ready for the end of the school year.

For King, it was especially disturbing that this ancient kingdom was the only real exploration of Black excellence and that conversations otherwise about Black history were focused on the misery and horror of slavery but not on the rebellions and escapes—not on the strength required to endure and resist. It contributed to making Blackness feel inferior and synonymous with negativity to him rather than portraying it in the full tapestry of both the horrors and the triumphs.

Ariya was an 18-year-old senior in a public high school in the Southeast, in a populous urban-suburban district. She described herself as biracial (Black and Puerto Rican)[39] and a high-achieving student. Like King, she was also unsatisfied with the representation of Black history in her school. Though she was in a different part of the country than King (Southeast versus Northeast), she had similar concerns about what was being taught (and not taught) in her classes. In sharp contrast with the middle school English teacher who made the learning environment productively "intellectually hazardous" but still "physically safe and personally respectful," Ariya had other teachers whose content thoroughly avoided hard conversations. In high school English classes, for instance, it was disappointing when "the teacher would shut [conversations] down the moment they got a little too controversial," the opposite of her experience in her engaging yet challenging middle school English class.

But it was even more of an issue when the content portrayed an incomplete or inaccurate story that avoided difficult truths about the past. As Ariya put it, "When you know something . . . and you get to the history class, and they don't talk about it, it's, one, disappointing; two, kind of scary; and three, removes all faith you have in your education system."

Ariya said she benefitted from having one friend who was an avid history buff, read a lot outside the classroom, and would share information beyond what was shared in class:

We got to the civil rights movement, and they were talking about how Martin Luther King Jr. was for peace, and Malcolm X was for violence, and Fred Hampton was killed in a raid because he shot at some guy and the dude shot back—I know my friend completely checked out. Because, one, that's just so surface level than what actually happened.[40] And then, two, he felt like they purposefully weren't giving us the whole truth, and I completely agreed with him. If I know [differently], . . . why would I want to sit here and watch the glamorization or the glorification of these historical figures? Especially like Christopher Columbus. They talked about how he discovered America, and we're just like, "[That] did not happen. He did not discover America." . . . And so, when you see it portrayed that way, it's scary. It's disappointing. And then you just, you're checked out; you don't want to listen. And so, it always made it a lot harder for me to learn. And then, when I know those things and then I have to talk and debate and have projects with my peers who don't know those things, it puts me in a precarious situation and a disadvantage.

Ariya continued to talk about all of the implications of approaching historical content in inaccurate ways to avoid political fallout:

I know it was a very big controversy . . . when they took a picture of one of the textbooks in Texas, and it showed the Trail of Tears as being completely willing instead of what it was. And when I hear that, I'm just like, "Okay, well, one, you're teaching this, and now these people are gonna grow up and vote, and I got to deal with that. And then, two, Why are you [teaching it that way]? . . . And three, is it hurting me not to tell me that?"

And so, if I come to the conclusion that it's hurting me, then that means the people who are running the school system are not only intentionally hurting me, but they know that, and they don't have my interests and my education in the forefront of their mind. . . . You're supposed to want that for me. And if you don't, it's just very scary, not only for me but for a whole generation of voters who are eventually going to vote someone in, and I'm going to have to deal with the repercussions of that.

Though we personally suspect most teachers and administrators don't realize how much they are hurting students by leaving out painful elements of history, Ariya's point still stands: parents, educators, administrators, and citizens are generally supposed to want the best quality education for students. Why else would our society invest in it as a public good? And while the culture wars raging around education currently have made the discussion of what does and doesn't get covered in class content a politically polarizing issue, it doesn't have to be treated that way.

Allowing the place of historical content and current events inside classrooms to stay a political issue means real consequences for students. For Ariya and her peers, for instance, it left them feeling like they had to choose between spending their time educating themselves to counter omissions and inaccuracies and spending their time on activities that would allow them to succeed in the college admission and preparation process:

I had to do a lot of work and a lot of extracurriculars and a lot of clubs, and a lot of just academic work as a whole just to set myself up as competitive for the school that I was going to apply to. So, if I do all of that, and I have school from six to two, and then I'd have to get home at three and then have a work call from three-thirty to six. And then I have to do schoolwork for my AP classes, and that'll take me six to nine. Then I have to shower and then have to get ready [for bed], and then have to do it all again. I don't really have the time to sit by and fact-check everything you're teaching me. So, I have to be complicit in the knowledge that this is probably not the whole story, and then also I don't have the time to get the whole story. So then there are my friends, like the one who's a complete history geek, who does know the whole story because . . . he spends so much time with history. And as a result, he doesn't spend as much time at school or doing the extracurriculars or the clubs, the jobs, the trainings, and seminars. And because of that, he's not as competitive for these really prestigious universities. But he probably knows a lot more than I do about these things. And so, it's like, I have to choose between what's important to me and [whether] to disadvantage myself. I have to sit in class and . . . be aware of the fact it's not the full story, but I don't have time to get the whole story. But my friend has the whole story, but because he didn't get the whole story at school, he's not doing as well, and so people don't take him seriously.

What is especially appalling about this double bind is that it's only a trap for students who genuinely want to learn, who care about their learning, and who want it to empower their participation in society. If that's not the student profile we are building up and rewarding through our educational systems and structures, then what are we doing? The modern workforce needs informed critical thinkers, not mindless automatons whose jobs can readily be replaced by programming. Yet the kind of system Ariya is describing is one that most rewards those who are willing to mindlessly follow along.

What to Do When Abilities Aren't Supported

So, what can we take away from all these stories of environments that stifled students' ability to learn? A few things, actually. The first is for adults to push ourselves to think about what abilities we really hope students will develop in school and whether we're inadvertently inhibiting those important abilities from flourishing by focusing on less important ones. For example, if you're a parent pushing your teen for a great-looking college resume, pause to think about the effect that has not only on their learning right now but also on their mental model for what will allow them to succeed and thrive in the future. If you're an educator with worried students, start by empathizing with their panic over grades rather than only being frustrated by it, and work with them to find a collaborative solution. And if you're a parent or an educator who is baffled by the seeming lack of interest and capacity for learning in some of the young people you know, check to see if there's anything in their current learning environment that might be making it feel much safer to not even try to develop an ability than to try and fail.

For adults and teens wondering how to rebuild a sense of competence that's been damaged, Layla shared an example of how she rebuilt her sense of competence that may help. Layla had to work hard to feel capable of succeeding in the STEM courses at her university, for all the reasons already discussed in prior chapters, and so it really hurt when her then-boyfriend said, "he felt like he was working harder than [her] in engineering":

> *I didn't realize I had completely based my worth on what he had said, even though I knew it wasn't true, and I knew that he most likely said that [not] with malice. Him saying that . . . meant that he also is projecting a sort of insecurity that he feels, like he has to be better. Like, we have to be top tier together. . . . So him projecting that onto me and making me feel the same way that I had already been feeling subconsciously just fried me that week. But I feel like, looking at it, months pass[ed], I realize[d] I'm not stupid. I just don't know [the content] yet. . . . And not*

knowing yet doesn't mean that I'm going to get it now, or the next time, or the next time. I'll get it at some point, or I won't, and that's okay.

Though she described her ex-boyfriend's comment as being the most immediate trigger that had caused her to so deeply question her ability to learn and succeed, it happened in the context of several other traumas that had unfolded in the preceding months: her mom had been in a serious accident, her grandparents had died suddenly, and she had experienced a sexual assault. All these experiences combined to leave her feeling like there was something uniquely wrong with her abilities and her life, especially because she had a binary mentality of "I need to be perfect, or what's the point?" It's common for trauma to deeply unsettle people's sense of who they are and what they're capable of, and it took Layla time and effort to develop the self-awareness and resilience to shift her view of herself to someone who can learn and just hasn't yet. Rebuilding a sense of ability that's been deeply shaken is not fast work, in other words, but it is possible.

Layla's reframe reminded us of the advice King said he would give younger students who are looking for ways to make school less painful:

Don't say, "Oh, I'm not good at math." Or "Oh, English is my least favorite subject." Because all those comments are putting a box around what you can and can't do. So. I like to say this, that "Oh, I don't know this yet." Always put a "yet" behind every "I don't know." Because that "yet" says that where you don't know now, that does not mean that you will not know later on.

In their descriptions, Layla and King simplify the most vital elements of Carol Dweck's famous research on "growth mindset" without ever using those words.[41] Believing one is capable of growth, both generally and in specific areas, is a crucial foundation for feeling motivated to learn, and choosing to see oneself as someone who just hasn't learned how to do something *yet* is a perfect way to build that sense of ability at a foundational level. To help the young people you care about build their sense of growth mindset, one of the most important things you can do is model it—which means uncovering where you have tended to act or talk in ways that make it clear you think of your own abilities, or theirs, as fixed, and shifting that behavior.

Believing in our capacity to grow and learn is vital not only for feeling capable in school but also for setting goals, a topic explored in the next chapter. Since most adults hope teens will set and pursue productive goals, it's worth pausing to think about the relationship between a student's sense of their abilities and the kinds of goals they will pursue. People don't set goals that require skills they think they're incapable of developing. If someone doesn't think they're good at math, they're not going to have a goal to become a physicist. If they think they're bad at English, they're unlikely to pursue any field that requires writing. And if they think they're bad at learning, it's going to be hard to have any goal at all—a challenge that affects any student who conflates how well they're doing in their particular *classes* with how capable they are of *learning* and, therefore, how successful they can become

Building students' feelings of competence is not the same as building a vapid sense of self-esteem—but it is crucial that, at this time of identity formation, they experience enough moments of their own capacity to learn to have that sense of ability (to *learn*, not to just be skilled at *performing*) baked into their view of who they are. Though claims that 85% of jobs that will exist in a decade haven't been invented yet are designed to grab headlines,[42] the pace of technological and cultural change means that the one skill we know will always be valuable is the capacity to learn and grow. If we fail to convey that capacity to young people now, we'll be making their futures much harder.

More Ideas From Experienced Practitioners

For Parents:

- Help your kids interrogate why they feel they can learn in some classes and can't learn in others. Structural causes, like poor curriculum choices, warrant advocacy at the district or state level, whereas interpersonal causes, like teacher overwhelm or burnout, benefit from interpersonal connection. And on the rare occasion when a teacher is genuinely just power-mad and cruel, the goal should be to diminish their effect on your teen's perception of themselves.

- Offer to help students who are struggling with a content area find another way to learn that content area if they really don't feel comfortable going to their teacher about it. There are often volunteer tutoring options available for those with financial constraints, or even just good video series online that explain difficult concepts. But, as with all the ideas throughout the book, don't force this help—it won't work anyway.

- If you feel like the biggest impediment to your teen's sense of ability is a lack of growth mindset, check out more resources on how to build it in both you and them, starting with Dweck's original book on the topic, *Mindset*. Don't leave yourself out of the equation here—you're more likely to be successful if you invest deeply in building this in yourself, thereby providing a model of what it looks like to recognize and shift this fundamental mentality, than if you try to get your teen to change their self-perception without ever changing your own. Chances are, if they're really steeped in a fixed mindset about certain abilities, you are, too.

For Educators:

- Make the purpose of assessment and homework clear to all involved. When the purpose is not clear, students feel like they are getting meaningless busywork, not building meaningful skills.

- Set students (and yourself) up for success. Success is reinforcing, and failure breeds failure (and apathy). Giving students the opportunity to succeed at something challenging but attainable will make them more likely to engage with more challenging material in the future.

6

Making It Meaningful

Relevance and Goals

"I'm sure people today would have gotten mad at my teacher for teaching me that, but I definitely think it was necessary. Learning, to me, is supposed to be very uncomfortable. It's supposed to really push you . . . past your limits."

- Ariya

"How can we tie this into different ideas that are used within the workplace in different fields? So, if we're teaching this math concept, how does that affect a student [who] wants to become a financial advisor? . . . Or how does that affect the student that wants to go into the arts . . . and have to kind of create their own arts business and make sure that they're marketable? Taking these very rudimentary concepts and saying, 'How do they affect people in their real lives?'"

- Connor

For abilities and choices to make a difference in motivation, they need to feel relevant. We only care about developing skills we believe we'll use, adults and teens alike. Similarly, choices matter a lot more when they are connected to something that matters to us or that we're interested in—picture a cafeteria where there's plenty of choice, but none of it matters because none of the dishes look appealing, or because you're simply not hungry yet.

Because so much of the relevance of school is based on the

premise it will be useful *later*, young people who have long-term goals usually find school easier to engage in than those who do not.[43] But, not all students have goals, and adults who try to push young people to develop their goals often end up just undermining their relationship with that young person instead. Trying to tackle goal selection head-on can be like pestering someone who isn't hungry about whether they want fish or chicken for dinner: They don't want to eat, they don't know why, they feel bad about not being hungry, and now they're also irritated with whoever is forcing the issue. Supporting young people in cultivating goals requires a more indirect approach to be successful.[44] [45]

We want to emphasize this risk up front before sharing all the interesting examples of our interviewees who had specific goals at the time we interviewed them and the difference it made in how they approached school. Otherwise, for those who currently don't have specific goals in mind, it's easy to read these examples as just another voice shouting about the importance of having a plan. Most young people already know they're "supposed" to have a plan, and more examples of why plans are so great likely won't do anything to help one spontaneously appear, especially if those examples feel like pressure. However, hearing others' stories in a "non-pressure way," to borrow Melanie's phrase, can spark ideas. And if they don't, adults can adopt approaches to content and activities that spark curiosity and exploration, which support both short-term learning and goal discovery.

Students with Long-Term Goals Find School More Relevant

Students who were pursuing long-term goals found meaning in more of their school activities. These goals contributed to their sense of direction, purpose, and motivation, leading to enhanced success and greater feelings of fulfillment. This aligns with what psychological research has shown for decades: pursuing goals, especially ones that are intrinsically valuable and oriented towards *learning* over *performance* (a.k.a. mastery-based, like the approach used by Layla's beloved high school chemistry teacher), predicts both academic success and overall well-being.[46]

Ava, Melanie, and Grace: Pursuing careers in medicine

When we asked Ava, "What keeps you going?" after she'd shared stories of frustration from her school experiences, she intertwined goals with what she believed to be her strengths. "My future career goal: I want to be a pediatrician. And I want to continue doing the things that these teachers are telling me that I've been doing [well], and I feel like pediatrics is the best way to do that. And it also works on my strengths of math and science." Melanie's goal of becoming a nurse also gave her focus:

> *My mom [has been] sick for most of my life. She was diagnosed with cancer when I was seven and then was re-diagnosed when I was in eighth grade. And she's in remission now, but from eighth to eleventh grade, she was in active treatment. And it was multiple cycles of it. And that was definitely an interesting time for me, I think. But I spent a lot of time in hospitals. And I got to see nurses work, and I really enjoyed not only the hands-on work that they did but also sometimes they would talk to me, and that made a really big, big impact on me.*

This is in keeping with what we've observed with other students, in and outside these interviews: exposure to new possibilities and meaningful experiences tend to do more to set and shape sustainable goals than external rewards or pressure. As Melanie noted, all her older sister's friends who had started off with pre-med majors to satisfy their parents ended up changing majors later on or changing career direction after they graduated.

Grace is also pursuing a medical career, one that intersects with her passion for writing and storytelling:

> *I was a sophomore in high school when my English teacher suggested that I speak to the high school's journalism and English teacher. She encouraged me to continue writing and take her journalism class the following semester, and I did. It ended up being one of my favorite courses in high school, and I started writing for my high school's online newspaper a year later. I worked up to being Editor-in-Chief during quarantine, and I learned a lot about myself: I love writing, and most importantly, I loved using storytelling to educate, advocate, and create empathy by sharing different perspectives. . . . Because I went to school in a predominantly Latine and Black community, I wrote about racial relations and used my personal stories to advocate for racial equity in education and inform my community on nation-wide and county-wide social issues that would most impact our community. I figured that I wanted to continue writing and educating communities, especially communities of color, on health topics that needed better explanations for laymen, so I decided to combine my goal of medicine with journalism.*

Since then, Grace said she continues to ask herself the same question she asked Ava: "'What keeps you going? Why medicine?' It's two simple questions, and I find myself adding on stories to further support my answer, and even though my long list of reasons keeps shifting and expanding, at the core, it's simple: I can't see myself doing anything else."

Like Melanie, Grace has had a closer and more personal encounter with the healthcare system than she would've liked. During the writing of this book, her father was diagnosed with cancer:

> *It felt like my worst nightmare came true. He is in his seventies, well-educated and distinguished, and a very supportive parent. He's also a lifelong learner—as a retired professor with a doctorate degree, he went back to school for a master's degree when I entered college because he was "tired of retirement." I never would've imagined having such a close encounter with medicine in this way, but I appreciate medicine and caregiving in a much more somber and deeper manner now. This experience enabled me to see past the seemingly more superficial reasons for medicine and internalize a deeper sense of what it meant to listen intently to patients, come up with a shared game plan for their health, and care for them.*

This experience has "intensified the significance of this goal" to Grace and made it that much more important in guiding what kinds of experiences both in and outside of school are most important to her.

Maria and Caprielle: Academic goals

Maria talked about how engaging most of her classes were for her because her college-prep- focused charter school's approach to the content was directly tied to their students' desire to get into college. Students at her school were allowed to start taking AP classes in ninth grade to begin building potential college credits, for instance. They also helped students start their college and scholarship searches early. They even assign students to begin writing personal statements more than a year before they'd need them for college applications "so we don't struggle with them." Additionally, she found her teachers frequently drew from "their experiences" to "talk about ways to deal with problems in college, or more emotional issues sometimes, like they did that a lot during the pandemic, or how to handle stress, and things like that."

She also appreciated that the teachers there consistently made expectations clear and pushed students to meet them by communicating things like, "Hey, you should be at this point. You should be doing your intro, or you should be researching this, or this timeline's supposed to be done." They'd "give tips, and it keeps people in line." This heightened focus on college preparedness was motivating for Maria because getting into college is a high-priority goal for her, and thus the demands of her school felt like support rather than unproductive pressure.

In a different way, Caprielle's experiences in school helped her develop both a sense of purpose and build broader academic goals. The purpose element came from seeing the strong contrast between the inclusivity of the school she attended for Kindergarten through eighth grade and the exclusionary environment in her high school:

> *[It affected] my morals and ethics, and what I want to do with my life, my sort of purpose, I guess, because a big part of the school was inclusion, which I now highly value, especially as someone who went to high school with this open attitude and inclusive personality, to seeing students that were so closed off if you weren't in their economic bracket or, if you didn't look like them. It [was] just, again, a very toxic culture. So, coming from a place that was so inclusive with so many diverse people and with disabilities and everything to go into that super small, not diverse environment was a big change and a big reason why I left [to try dual-enrollment classes at a local community college].*

Being able to be successful in that fully online, more independent environment gave her the confidence to then pivot to being fully in the dual-enrollment program, Running Start, rather than just taking some college credit classes while staying in high school:

> *I realized that I can really just do this on my own, my high school experience. I want to prioritize my academics, and I know that this is going to propel me toward a better future for myself and my family, and what I can do now to help my future is what my goal is. So, just learning that independence and learning that I'm okay alone, and I'm okay without a "best friend" was really what drove me to be like, "Yeah, I'll do dual enrollment." It seems like the best bet, and I'm going a little ahead, but when I graduate with college credits and I likely go to a school in my state, I can most likely graduate within two years with my intended major. So, that's obviously a huge plus to propel my education even further so I can go pursue other things or goals.*

Her story has similarities with Eddie's. Like Caprielle, he was relieved "to be free of . . . having to uphold a certain [social] facade." Eddie doubled down on plowing through his required courses while COVID-19 gave him the opportunity to do them online so he could do entirely hands-on, in-person electives his senior year. Caprielle used the opportunity to stay online to build her confidence that she could manage a full dual-enrollment set of courses. For both of them, the opportunity to do school their way built up their interest and confidence in pursuing their goals.

For Caprielle, these choices also shifted her take on why it mattered to her to do well in school:

> *I think for my whole life, it was very "[prioritize] academics because you should want it"—like, you should want good grades, you should be the teacher's pet. . . . That wasn't my family's pressure, and that wasn't the school's pressure; it was really just my perception of being a student. . . . So, now that I'm in college,*

and I'm finding out what I like about myself and what I want my career path to be, and where I want to go, what I want my future to be like, I really have this sense of "I want to get good grades for me." You know, it's not that pressure of what a student should be; it's what I want myself to be.

Caprielle's example reminded us that goals don't always have to be crystal clear career goals to be motivating and make school more engaging. Simply having a reason to invest in some aspect of school that feels personally motivating, rather than like an external "should," is enough to energize and provide lasting motivation.

Connor: "I was able to problem-solve, and that made it interesting."

Connor's story illustrates another good reminder about goals: they don't have to stay the same to be motivating and provide focus:

Watching . . . that project [Coping with COVID] grow and evolve and learning more and more about social sciences and sociology and how we understand the world—I really love doing that work. I really love learning more about my community and my peers and the people [who] made it up. And so that kind of furthered me to look more at the social sciences in general as a place that I could be more academically focused. And I've been able to take some interesting classes exploring that a bit more and beefing up my skills and doing similar projects. And so, I've been very happy with that.

Discovering new academic interests through this project was also helpful to Connor because "the pandemic, when it started in March, forced [him] to really reevaluate [his] interest in computer science":

> I had always said that I wanted to do it for a very long time. I was always very gung-ho, [saying] since I was like six years old, "I want to work with computers, I want to do computer science, I want to be a programmer," even when I didn't really understand what that meant. I knew I wanted to do it. And so, I just kind of kept saying it. And as I did some work, I enjoyed it. But it didn't—I wasn't necessarily attracted to it, especially in the same way that I was with some of the more social sciences work. And I couldn't figure out why.

For many people, whether adolescents or adults, discovering they're no longer interested in something they'd previously identified with and spent a lot of time and energy on would be disorienting. Connor, however, decided to use the dual-enrollment program as an opportunity to really delve into his growing questions:

> So, as I came into this dual enrollment program, one of the questions that they asked [was], "What are some fields that you're interested in?" and one of the things that I actually put down was biotechnology. Just because it was kind of on a whim, I was like, "Oh, this idea of taking computer science and taking biology together seems neat; I would like to know more about it." So, I put it down as an option. And I got introduced to a program here at Western Kentucky University that kind of takes very early undergraduate students through the process of biology, research and bioinformatics, and biotechnology . . . and trying to uncover genes and understand more about viruses. So that program kind of launched me both on the in-lab and on-the-computer sides of biology and how we understand that. And so, more specifically, I'm not just interested in biology; I'm interested in bioinformatics and the way that we disentangle the data from

biology and how we can use that to uncover new things. And so that exploration is something that I've also done during my time here at Western. I've really, really loved it. It's been a process going through that, but I really haven't looked back. And at the same time, I've really been able to reignite my enjoyment of computer science, taking more classes in it, having more structure with it, being able to focus on different projects, and even do a bit of research with it.

He set a goal for himself to explore more possibilities, ignited by his experience with KSVT in discovering that he liked the social sciences, an area he'd previously dismissed. Having a goal to explore is different than aimless drifting—both can lead to rewarding discoveries, but the former usually feels more motivating along the way.

This open-minded exploration also helped Connor discern what elements of computer sciences still interested him. Before Western Kentucky University, his exposure to computer science had increasingly felt "stifled," "more kind of being 'help desk,' being the guy that knows how technology works and how to engage with it. And then I would do a little bit of small programming things on the side . . . things like 'hour of code' . . . where it's really basic programming." He felt he wasn't able to solve real problems with these kinds of activities, but at Western Kentucky, he found his classes took a different approach, where within a single class, they started with the basics but then rapidly moved into solving real problems with code:

Those types of ideas and that type of problem-solving, beyond just very basic experimentation, was something that I got really interested in, that pushed me forward with computer science more here than what I was doing in the past. . . . I was able to problem solve, and that made it interesting. . . . That's what excites me about computer science, is having a limited toolset

and figuring out how all the pieces fit together. And then apply-
ing that to a problem in a certain field, whether that be the
social sciences, biology, or something else entirely.

If Connor had simply given up on his computer science goals completely, he wouldn't have had this realization. But he also wouldn't have had it if he'd just kept doing the same kind of repetitive coding opportunities he'd been presented with as a high schooler that had begun to bore him. Getting curious about what he could explore that might allow him to connect his earlier interests in computer science with his growing interests in other fields gave him a different kind of goal, one that motivated him to stay engaged without narrowing his options too soon.

King, Nina, and Zimo: Making practical choices that leave room for your goals

We shared part of King's advice to younger students, about attaching a "yet" to any "I don't know," a few pages ago. Following that piece of advice for younger students, he also shared that "sometimes you're gonna have to take courses that sometimes you don't like. Sometimes, you may take a course in astronomy when you're really shooting for law. But those times where you need to do stuff that you don't want to do, [approach it] with an open mind. Don't put yourself in a box or automatically check out." This practical advice reminded us of Nina's and Zimo's stories, even though their practicality was about choosing courses and programs rather than mindsets.

Nina, for instance, decided that she didn't want to enter college until she knew exactly why she'd be incurring that debt and investing that time. So, as we mentioned before, she waited until she was 19 to begin, two years after she'd finished her high school diploma at 17. Though she knew she wanted to get a four-year degree eventually, she deliberately chose to start at a two-year college because it was a far more cost-efficient way of getting the first two years of school done. This also shaped her decision on what four-year college to transfer to as she drew closer to completing her associate's degree. The honors program she participated in at her two-year school meant she was eligible for scholarships to two other four-year schools in her state. But since her "end goal is law school," she picked the program that also fed into a law school and provided "a financial incentive to go to [their] Law School." As Nina summed it up, "I saw that path as making more sense."

Where Nina made practical choices about how to reach her goals in financially responsible ways, Zimo made practical choices about courses to take in his dual-enrollment program to maximize transferable credits. "I took a course in probability, which, I have to be entirely honest, I took that class with the primary motivation of it transferring as a course that is specifically recognized by [my desired university] as a requirement for their computer science degree." Though the primary motive was practical, the course was still "engaging, because it talks about concepts that I'm interested in . . . things like probability. I wanted to learn about them for a long while, and I didn't get to learn until now. So, I'm very happy about learning it."

The course on probability was not the only one Zimo selected for transferability. Though his academic goal is to major in computer science, he deliberately took a number of courses outside this immediate area as part of his dual-enrollment program:

> I wouldn't say they're direct skills, but I would say they're mostly there for me to expand my breadth. As in to learn more about different types of things than it being directly helpful to career advancement. So, the thing with [the dual-enrollment university's] computer science is that it won't transfer anything to [my

desired university] after the first semester, or basically anywhere else. So, instead of doing a lot of computer science, I chose to spend a year just exploring the different math classes.

In order to make sure he stays engaged with computer science during this time, he, along "with a few other people from the program," runs the computer science club.

Even a Chinese calligraphy class that he expected to find both boring and irrelevant when he was a younger student and then ended up finding useful was for practical reasons:

"How to write Chinese." It's not glamorous, [not] the artistic writing that people use as a form of art, but for the scope of the class, it's really just to help you write Chinese in a more readable way. And I expected it to be boring and useless. It was boring, but that turned out to be not so useless because, you see, when you wrote those Chinese exams, they're gonna make you write six hundred to a thousand characters worth of an essay for every exam, plus a number of reading comprehension questions for which you have to write something on the page. . . . Writing in legible handwriting quickly is extremely helpful in that regard. . . . It also turned out to serve as sort of a cultural bond because calligraphy is something you can talk [about] to other people of Chinese backgrounds, and you can expect them to at least know something about it.

This point of connection made the class that was originally boring feel much "less boring" in retrospect. His description of this experience seems like an illustration of King's advice to keep an open mind—though Zimo expected to find this required class both boring and useless, he first discovered its usefulness and later even an opportunity for interesting connections from it, that he wouldn't have had access to if he had simply put himself "in a box." In this, King's advice and Zimo's experience echo the idea of choosing how to respond discussed in the chapter on choice and illuminate the delicate balance between making the most of just being assigned to something and feeling like one can make choices that support, or at least make room for, one's goals.

Exposure to New Possibilities Can Prime Goal Development

We've referenced the research on developmental relationships before, but it's worth briefly revisiting. One of the five characteristics of a developmental relationship—and the one researchers have found to be least common in relationships between adults and young people—is the act of "expanding possibilities."[47] Expanding possibilities includes three actions: broadening someone's horizons by exposing them to "new ideas, experiences, and places;" inspiring them to "see possibilities" for their future; and introducing them to people who can help them grow personally, academically, or professionally. Decades of research show that when young people have adults in their lives who not only provide care and support (qualities exemplified by many of the stories already shared in this chapter) but also increase their sense of what's possible in their lives, those young people are more likely to be engaged in school, graduate, and thrive.

Mirroring the finding that this element is less common in relationships between young people and adults, our interviewees less often shared stories about educators who exposed them to new ideas and possibilities or introduced them to people who would help them grow. When they did, however, those moments had an especially large impact. Connecting students with new possibilities didn't need to stay in a teacher's subject area, either. For example, Layla's chemistry teacher gave a "recommendation [that] got me into the summer program with the ACLU for civil liberties, and it . . . opened my mind a lot more to political issues and made me so much more politically aware." Elena's math teacher was actually the one who wrote her a recommendation to get into a summer art program she was interested in, which allowed her to really pursue the study of art seriously, something the electives in her school system lacked. And, as the stories below illustrate, being connected to people and possibilities that either weren't previously on a young person's radar at all or felt like a distant and unlikely pipe dream can spark a sense of potential and purpose that wasn't previously there. If nurtured, that new possibility can grow into a goal.

Eddie: "Being there was very new to me, and it just got me really excited."

Eddie's business teacher expanded possibilities for students by introducing them to new people and new experiences. In addition to engaging them with her enthusiasm and creativity, she also created opportunities for students to get involved in activities outside her classroom. One of those opportunities included a chance to volunteer at a "business start-up event" one weekend, where "all these entrepreneurs pitch their ideas to some investors." Eddie's description made it very clear just how much this one event expanded his horizons:

> It was one of the best things I've done in my life. . . . I've never been to anything like that. I've never been around that environment. . . . So being there was very new to me, and it just got me really excited. It was cool because a lot of the people there were more than willing to talk. And while we were there, we got to walk around the stands and talk to the entrepreneurs. And some of them were doing really well, and they were just there for the connections. Like, some of them did not need the cash prize, and I was like, "Wow, that's kind of cool."

While there, he met one entrepreneur in particular:

I was just talking to one of the guys, and . . . it's not like he was anyone special. And he was telling me, "You know, I wasn't far from where you are, at your age." It was cool to see how maybe this is possible, you know; being able to get to this level one day is a possibility.

This matches the research: When young people see themselves in others and see them do surprising and inspiring things, it opens up their imagination of what's possible in their own lives, allowing them to set and pursue new or bigger goals.

When I asked him how that conversation with the entrepreneur started, he said it began with the entrepreneur explaining the app he was developing. This created the first point of connection since, at the time, Eddie had also begun developing apps. The entrepreneur's app was related to parents being able to keep track of their kids' sporting events when they couldn't be at the game live. Then, as Eddie put it, "We got into talking about what we did in high school, and he's like, 'Yeah, I played sports too.' We just started talking, and I was like, 'Wow, you know, we're not that different.' . . . His experience of his childhood was sort of like mine." In other words, Eddie saw enough overlap to make a possibility he had previously only wondered about—that of becoming a successful programmer and entrepreneur—feel like a real option for him. That dream began to feel like something he could actually achieve if he was willing to sustain "motivation and hard work" like this entrepreneur whose background was similar to his own. And none of this increased sense of possibility would have happened if his teacher hadn't first built a relationship with Eddie where he trusted her suggestions and then connected Eddie to the opportunity to volunteer at this entrepreneurial event.

Caprielle: "It made me change perspective."

Educators can also expand students' perception of themselves by the responsibilities they give them. For example, when Caprielle was in middle school, she was well-known by her teachers and the school administrator because the school was a fairly small private school she'd been attending since elementary. As a result, they saw potential in her she hadn't previously seen in herself:

> *There was a younger girl with Down syndrome. The lunchroom just became a little too chaotic for her, so my best friend and I were asked to have lunch with her every day for that full year. It was seventh grade, so it was kind of like the prime social time, I guess. . . . I didn't make any other new friends [that year] when there were girls that I was curious about getting to know. . . . I realized later, "Oh wow, I could be doing what these other girls are doing. I could be at lunch every day talking about what we're going to do that weekend or what clothing that we like." [It] made me change perspective on that [experience], like, "Wow, they see me as someone who can hold a lot of responsibility." And then eighth grade came, and the girl wanted to go back out to the lunchroom to make friends, and I realized that my time away from my classmates didn't hinder me. I don't regret staying with her at all that year. . . . It's just I feel like I've grown . . . so I'm really grateful for that.*

The adults in Caprielle's school prompted her to see herself in a new way because they exposed her to the opportunity to take on a different kind of responsibility in their school community. By doing that, they prompted her to realize how much she valued and wanted to be a part of inclusive environments, which contributed to her resolve to step away from her non-inclusive high school environment and immerse herself fully in the dual-enrollment program at her community college.

Goals Are Not the Only Path to Relevance

While long-term goals make it easier to engage in school, many high-school-aged young people don't yet have goals in mind for their later academic or professional life despite increasingly feeling like they're supposed to. The pressure to have academic goals often starts in elementary school, and by high school, the pressure increases to have one's academic goals tied to a career goal. That pressure not only feels overwhelming for some students, but it can also make the feeling of aimlessness and irrelevance in school even greater because it seems like academic content is only meant for people who do have academically related goals. This can feel like an impossible double-bind—if goals help, but we can't directly push someone into a goal, what can be done to make school not suck for those without goals? As the stories in the last section illustrate, the long-game move is to keep exposing young people to new ideas and opportunities.[48] But in the short term, any focus on making class content more relevant to students can help.

Avery, Ava, and Ian: Relevance via hands-on activities

Ava had a physics teacher, for instance, who "definitely changed the way" she looks at the world through science:

> *There's a lot of things that you really don't know about the world, and that's what physics is: the way the world works behind just what you see. Like, we did this thing where we used a mirror when we were learning about lenses, and when we used a*

mirror, just looking in the mirror, trace something, and see how that just disrupts your perspective. And I'd say we do a lot of activities like that that just make you think. It just makes it so fun to learn about the world.

Similarly, Ian's economics teacher "always had games to play, but the games always related to what we were learning." In particular, he described one activity that stood out in his memory:

We made a stock-market-type of graph on the ground. And we used our bodies to represent the different parts of the graph, so we had to lie down. It would be like the first person to lay where he says [would get points], so he'd be like, "Lay on the bounding line." And then you'd have to be the first one to lay there. So that we can memorize the different parts of the graph.

And Avery also talked about how physically engaging activities made a difference in his learning:

My seventh-grade math teacher, he would always engage . . . us as much as he could. We did like fun projects. . . . [For example,] he would make us get up and walk around the room, [and] there were problems around the room that we had to solve. Whoever got done with them first got, like, a little treat or whatever. . . . And my chemistry teacher, he engages with the class; it's easy to follow along. He teaches [so that] it's just way easier to care about the class . . . like he'll come around the class and show us different elements and stuff or do cool little examples. . . . It's just they made the class fun, even if it's not fun. Overall, school isn't meant to be fun, right? But they made it fun.

Though these kinds of activities weren't especially complex, they stood out to students as memorable, engaging, and effective at helping them retain or apply information they otherwise would have struggled to recall, much less apply.

Avery also illustrated why it's important for even fun activities to still feel related to present or future usefulness when we asked him if any teachers had tried to make class fun, like his math and chemistry teachers had, and failed. He noted that his Spanish teacher tried to do game-like activities but that it still didn't engage him. "If I know I'm never going to use it ever, I can't be bothered to try so hard. I can tell that she does try. . . . It's just not fun. Maybe some of the other kids find it fun." This was the case even though Avery didn't have any specific career goals yet. "I don't plan on doing any-thing with a lot of the subjects. . . . I'm not really sure what I'm going to do." In the meantime, having engaging activities around something that at least seems possibly useful in the future provides some of the same benefits clear goals provide: it boosts engagement and focus. It also can create space for interests, and then goals, to eventually emerge, similar to how Goose described her goals around excelling in English emerg-ing from her earlier success in those classes.

Goose and Ariya: "Challenging us to think deeper."

Games and physical movement aren't the only way to make course content feel more engaging and relevant. Goose talked about a Spanish course she particularly appreciated:

For all of the Spanish courses I've taken in my life, it's like gram-mar, reading, and doing units on history or whatever, but this year, we really employed the usage of the Spanish language, and suddenly, we weren't talking about grammar as much, we were having conversations about ethical stuff and history in Spanish, so that made it really fun. . . . He would do a lot of assignments that were interesting, so we were researching art by modernists, we were analyzing the work in Spanish, and he also asked us questions . . . [about] advancing civilization, about technology. . . . He was just asking us real-world questions, "What do you think?" questions, and always challenging us to think deeper.

Whereas games can be a great way of building basic skills—much like commercial language acquisition apps often do—using growing abilities to engage deeply in new ways of thinking creates a much more meaningful and relevant way to continue to deepen those abilities.

Making content more engaging by drawing students into meaningful and challenging conversations was an even stronger motivator for Ariya. She shared a story about a middle school English class where they read the book *Getting Away with Murder: The True Story of the Emmett Till Case*:

Now that I'm thinking of it, you know, there's so many conversations about "Should ninth-graders be allowed to read certain books?" that are a lot less grisly than the details of that, so I'm sure people today would have gotten mad at my teacher for teaching me that, but I definitely think it was necessary. "Learning," to me, is supposed to be very uncomfortable. It's supposed to really push you to your limits and push you past your limits. And that was probably the first lesson where I was like, Yeah, this is pushing me past my limit. I don't know if I like this at all. And I wasn't meant to like it. I don't. It was really hard to sit and kind of have that conversation not only with my Black peers but [also with] my White peers. This happened. It was really gross. It didn't happen that long ago. It didn't need to happen. It shouldn't have happened. And those were like concrete facts, but then we got into the kind of nitty-gritty details of it. Okay, is it acceptable for us to defend Southern heritage at the cost of a little boy, really? And then, of course, we got into the more modern details of "how does that affect us now? Although lynchings may not be as grisly as they were back then, how do hate crimes still persist today?" I think there was a question: "Is there such a thing as Black privilege?" And really, it was definitely uncomfortable. I was definitely annoyed and mad, probably that whole unit. But we're supposed to have those conversations. It was supposed to be uncomfortable. It was supposed to be cringe-worthy, and I'm sure parents would have wanted us to censor the picture. But it was important for us not only to read it but [also] see the aftermath.

Although Ariya's perspectives about this teacher and her approach to this class—and the negative consequences of the approach other teachers took, when they avoided difficult conversations and taught only banal facts—are discussed more in the previous chapter, it was important to us to include Ariya's commentary here in order to expand the sense of what kinds of activities can make a classroom environment feel more relevant, engaging, and meaningful. Ariya's story shows how learning becomes more relevant if it pushes you to be productively uncomfortable, to wrestle with hard questions that matter not because they are tied to an individual goal but because they connect to being human in a given culture at a given time.

Connor: "How do they affect people in their real lives?"

Connor also talked about ways he saw certain approaches to content used by the professors in his dual-enrollment program make required coursework feel more useful. We asked him if it wasn't just the more elective nature of college classes that allowed him to feel greater relevance in those experiences. While acknowledging that universities and colleges "have the advantage of having students that are more apt to be engaged, because . . . they're going to get a degree, and they're paying," he still didn't fully agree with our hypothesis:

I want to push back against that a little bit. . . . Even for the universities that have the most strict general education requirements, they're often able to tie those general education requirements into the concept of a certain degree. So, for example, the physics class I'm taking currently is something I have to take as a general education requirement. . . . It's just something you have to do. But the class is applicable to [anyone] in the STEM fields, all at the same time, by connecting them with different concepts. And so, I think where high schools can kind of take a note from that . . . is by saying, "How can we tie this into different fields?"

Connor acknowledged that "of course, you're going to have a greater diversity of students that are going to go into a greater diversity of things" in a general high school class. But he still felt educators and curriculum designers could ask themselves useful questions like:

How can we tie this into different ideas that are used within the workplace in different fields? So, if we're teaching this math concept, how does that affect a student [who] wants to become a financial advisor? . . . Or how does that affect the student that wants to go into the arts . . . and have to kind of create their own arts business and make sure that they're marketable? Taking these very rudimentary concepts and saying, "How do they affect people in their real lives?"

He further acknowledged that "sometimes the answer to that's going to be 'it doesn't.'" But he had ideas on how that dilemma could be approached as well.

For example, "not every student needs Algebra 2" for their future work,[49] "but they'll still need the skills to think logically and to use complex concepts and use numbers to get to a solution. That's something that everyone needs to know how to do." In general, he argued it would help tremendously if teachers would explain things like, "Here's what you should be pulling from this class, and here's how it's going to be affecting you for the rest of your life":

> *Making that clear up front, like a lot of university courses do, is something that I think is really, really special. And when I've seen that happen in my high school classes, before doing this dual enrollment program, I felt more engaged, and being here, it's very clear to see the trajectory of these classes and how they connect together, and how they connect to a larger career field for my life, and to see that future for myself, which I know is a struggle for a lot of students. . . . But being able to see that future and see how my education fits into that is really, really import- ant. I think it's something that high schools could do.*

Connor's experiences illustrate one way of helping students see a trajectory between what they're doing now and what they'll be doing in the future, even for students with only vague ideas of what their future interests are.

Brian: "You need to be able to learn the relevance of what you're learning."

Similar to Avery and Connor, Brian also saw relevance as crucial to improving the experience of school, and he saw it as something for both students and teachers to take action on. Brian, a 19-year-old who had begun high school in public school and shifted to a private online academy, described himself as bi-racial (Asian and White) and on the autism spectrum. For Brian, a sense of relevance was missing for most of his high school experience, which contributed to his uncertainty about what path to pursue next. When asked what advice he'd give to younger students, he said, "You need to be able to learn the relevance of what you're learning." He added:

At the same time, that also means teachers and the curriculum needs to know what's relevant and what's not so they can cut it out [and] make more time for the useful information. And hurt students less with unnecessary information that they're forced to learn that can make their grade suffer and that could just ruin their mentality for classes.

Brian's advice shows a crucial connection between relevance and abilities: If something seems useless, it's hard to learn—but if students have repeated experiences of school content being hard to learn, that quickly evolves into a mindset that they're not good at school, which inhibits future learning even more.

Whereas Connor advised that classes could become more relevant by tying them to future life and work as an adult, Brian suggested a different approach:

What would probably help is if you could make connections; that would be useful. And ways it could be interesting. Not like, "Oh, think of it this way" or "later on in life" [connections]. Those really don't help a lot of kids. Really [connections to] more immediate interests.

Connor's advice would likely work well for students with a strong future orientation, but Brian's advice is more likely to work for students who not only don't have a specific longer-term goal already but don't even have a strong sense of the kind of future life they want to live.

Caprielle: "We have a life outside school."

Caprielle prompted us to think about another important way for adults and teens to shift their thinking about the place of school in young people's lives:

I want the other generations to know . . . that we have a life outside school. It's not said, but it's underlying that school is just our whole lives. Whether I go to the orthodontist, or the doctor, or wherever, the first thing that's asked [is], "How's high school going?" It's just such an easy conversation. And they're right to think that, because it utterly consumes our entire life, because you go to school for seven hours a day, and then you do extracurriculars, or sports, or clubs, and then you go home, and you do five hours of schoolwork. So, it does consume every aspect of our life. But I just wish that, even with classmates, I wish people would understand that people have struggles outside of school, especially for people in low-income households. There are students with circumstances that require them to have jobs, or maybe they have to provide for their family [in some other way]. I think those things prepare you for the "real world" more than school is doing.

This is not only true for young people who have significant responsibilities outside of school due to particularly demanding circumstances. No one deserves to have who they are be conflated with what they do, and this is especially important to remember during adolescence, a key time of identity formation.

Though it might be counter-intuitive—how can minimizing the importance of school help make it feel more relevant?—we put Caprielle's advice in this chapter because expanding the view of identity beyond just school can be helpful for both academically successful and less successful students, albeit for different reasons. Expanding "high-achiever" focus beyond school to anchor their identity in a vision of themselves that isn't only about how well they performed but about the whole of who they are could help decrease stress and shift the focus from just achieving to reflecting on what kind of growth and learning is actually meaningful to them. Conversely, for students who are less successful academically, expanding their view of who they are and what matters in their life may make it easier to find places where they can engage in school, even if they're small. If being a student is just one part of who you are, rather than the most important part, then it's safer to acknowledge that part isn't doing well and to exert effort in trying to get better instead of becoming apathetic as a way of protecting yourself from feeling incapable or overwhelmed. It's easier for anyone to grow if they don't believe that being good at that one thing is the only possible way to their success in life; learning happens best when the stakes are neither too low nor too high.

What to Do to Help Young People Find Relevance in School

Whether it's an adult talking with a young person or a young person's internal dialogue with themself, engaging in conversations about goals and skills from a place of compassionate curiosity, rather than "we need to fix this problem," can be difficult. Melanie, for instance, described how she was frustrated that teachers only checked in with her when she "sought them out" and that she only sought them out because she was "really struggling" emotionally. She then said, "I think it's really hard . . . to find adults who care about you in a way that isn't like, 'Oh, let me check in with you. If you're good, you're great.' And that's it. . . . Like, 'I don't actually care about how you're doing; it's just we want to solve this issue.'" This feeling, that someone just wants to fix the "issue" of not having goals rather than be genuinely invested in the person, is one that students often get when the conversation of having goals comes up at home or at school. Instead, if you can be curious and promote their curiosity, you're more likely to be successful.

The stories in this chapter illustrate a few useful ways of avoiding this trap of trying to tackle goals head-on with students who don't have them. Ava, Ian, and Avery's stories show

how just making learning activities more hands-on can bolster engagement and leave space for goals to emerge. Goose and Ariya show how important wrestling with ideas and applying them to current life can make otherwise abstract skills or history feel meaningful right now. Connor demonstrates how required courses can become more relevant if the skills are tied to futures young people can actually imagine for themselves, and Brian's advice to help students find connections to immediate interests rather than abstract futures is another way to boost the relevance of schoolwork. Finally, Caprielle's advice for adults to step back and engage with young people as humans with lives outside just their role of "student" makes space for young people to situate the place of school in their overall identity, which could leave room for a clearer purpose to emerge.

More Ideas From Experienced Practitioners

For Families:

- Consider a few alternate ways to support relevance besides goal-setting that might work for your teen. For some, it works to focus on taking pride in the process of learning itself, such as the feeling of satisfaction in completing assignments or studying and finding deliberate ways of celebrating that progress. For others, getting support and encouragement from adults (or peers) can help. Finally, in all this, it's easy to forget how often young people, like adults, forget to prioritize basic self-care like getting enough sleep, healthy food, and exercise and making time for activities that bring joy and relaxation. Without doing that, it's hard to find the energy to engage in any challenge.

- Resist the pressure of working toward "perfection" and toward reaching the goal, no matter what. Otherwise, young people (and adults!) miss the joy of the journey, the joy of making mistakes and having the mistake lead to a new idea, or the joy of incremental gains and improvement. When no mistakes are made, there can be no happy accidents.

- Remember that the act of setting goals is important because that gives a person something to aim for; however, goals are meant to be changed, revised, and the process should not be complete torture. If the government can amend the Constitution, you can amend the goals you set for yourself!

- Encourage young people to dive into an interest rather than sitting back and waiting for "the best" answer. Waiting for the one true goal leads to inaction, hesitancy, and missing out on a potential "good enough" solution. Trying to find "the best" or "the right" answer about goals and careers lends itself to analysis paralysis, as most people could be successful in a variety of pursuits. Rather, go with what brings the most sense of purpose or passion right now and dive in. There is always an opportunity to revise later, and in the meantime, they were able to learn something interesting.

- Maintaining both unrelenting positive regard and a questioning stance (tips from prior chapters) can also help interactions to successfully shape goals. For example, if someone has bad eyesight, but their goal is to be a fighter pilot (a biologically impossible goal), start by questioning why that goal is appealing to them. Then, encourage self-reliance by having that person research the criteria for becoming a fighter pilot. Lastly, work with that person to help figure out other ways that they can achieve a similarly appealing goal that allows them to emphasize their strengths.

For Educators:

- Give yourself some grace. The likelihood that at least some of your students think your class is irrelevant and dull is high; it's almost inevitable in a low-choice environment like school. It won't help you or your students if you let that cause you to constantly beat yourself up or, on the flip side, become hardened to student opinion entirely. Focus on compassion for yourself and your students equally and treat them as collaborators in making the classroom more engaging for everyone (yourself included!). For example, ask your students what would make the boring parts of class interesting. Make it a playful game of "what if," where no idea is too wild to consider. If they can begin to come up with ideas on how to make dull content more interesting, and you use some of those ideas, they'll be more bought in even if the new ideas are a flop, and you'll have reduced the pressure on yourself to be the one responsible for coming up with solutions to their engagement. If they won't do this as a full class, consider that there's not enough belonging there yet, and try activities that build belonging first (see Chapter 2) and then return to this kind of activity.

- Remember why representation matters. Future career choices are influenced not just by subject matter but by the passion, excitement, and engagement of particular teachers. When this influence is profound, the impact can be lifelong and career-altering. This is why representation is particularly important, as it allows students to imagine someone like themselves in these positions. You can advocate for representation when your school is hiring new teachers, and you can also bring it in through guest speakers, field trips, and other forms of experiential learning.

What Else?

7

Tempting Distractions

Screen Time and Its Effects on Motivation

"I think it's an obvious fact that [we] grew up with smartphones and technology and, yes, I can probably work the interface of Snapchat and Instagram better than my grandma, of course. But I don't think the older generations understand the repercussions of growing up in that environment, surrounded by technology."

- Caprielle

"I don't want to touch social media because I know that if I do, I'm going to get caught up in stuff that I don't need to be getting caught up with."

- King

"It feels like there are a lot of teachers who feel obligated to do tech, but technology doesn't necessarily help anything, students aren't more engaged ... if anything it puts a hindrance on it, even for the good things technology does, where just having it available ... can be a way to disengage from education."

- Connor

One topic that is top of mind for almost every parent and educator of teens is the effect of screen time on not just teens' academic motivation but their lives overall. There are two areas of screen use that are most concerning to parents: video games and social media. The latter is especially concerning to parents because it's so new—while the internet was in its early stages when many current parents of teens were themselves teens, the ability to share thoughts, images, and videos for immediate response from anyone online was not. And the effects of these technologies on motivation are real: dopamine production, a key neurochemical in motivation and goal pursuit, is triggered by screen use,[50] and increased screen use correlates with decreased academic motivation.[51] It means we can get quick hits of pleasure from very little effort, making us more inclined to seek out that easy access in the future rather than seeking it from higher-effort activities like learning, growth, and goal-pursuit. And that means that for any adults invested in supporting young people's academic motivation, paying attention to when and how they use screens matters.

For most families, this is not as simple as just shutting down the screens. They're not only prevalent in contemporary society; mobile devices have increasingly become unavoidable within school and extracurriculars themselves. Parents we spoke with described how their kids were expected to follow club Instagram accounts and like a certain number of posts per week, download apps such as WhatsApp, GroupMe, and Slack to know when club or sports events were happening, and use laptops and tablets in class to engage with various school platforms for in-class polls, practice sessions, and homework. For any parent with a teen in public school, complete screen elimination isn't achievable.

Plus, not all recreational screen use is necessarily bad. In February 2023, the Chief Science Officer of the American Psychological Association, Dr. Mitch Prinstein, addressed Congress about both the positive potential and the damaging effects that the use of internet-based technology, especially social media, has on young people.[52] Prinstein discusses a few potential benefits of social media and other internet-based communication platforms—namely that they can be used to both build and maintain friendships and that the ability to keep in touch through messaging platforms made a positive difference to many young people, specifically during the COVID lockdown. He also pointed out that it can allow young people "to interact with a more diverse peer group"[53] than they would encounter offline and that digital spaces can provide an especially "important space for self-discovery and expression for LBGTQ+ youth."[54] Finally, he notes that there is some evidence that "youth are more likely to engage in civic activism online" and that this may be an effective place to engage young people in therapeutic interventions, especially in areas they feel self-conscious initiating with someone in person.

However, most of Prinstein's remarks addressed the significant risks, especially of social media. Many of these come from a simple matter of sequencing in how our brains develop from age 10 to age 25. (The APA focused on this broad age range because, other than the first year of life, it's the time when the most brain development is occurring.) At the start of this window, we develop the desire for "social rewards" (things like getting noticed and approved of by our peers), but it's not until the end of this window that we fully develop our ability to resist temptations. As Prinstein put it, this basically means that "when it comes to youths' cravings for social attention, they are 'all gas pedal with no brake.'"[55] This is a particular problem because the most used and promoted features of social media (things like number of likes, reshares, and views) "exploit this biological vulnerability among youth" and "capitalize on youths' biologically based need for social rewards."[56] In doing this, social media platforms are essentially equivalent to having candy instead of a meal, with similarly predictable effects—it removes the hunger for healthy peer connectedness by superficially filling that hunger, but in reality, it leaves people feeling more lonely and disconnected.

Social media profits from adolescents' desire for peer connection and approval while actually directing their behavior away from genuinely fulfilling that need. Instead, these platforms make it more likely for young people to engage in behaviors that harm themselves or others because of how algorithmic systems work to promote those attention-grabbing kinds of posts. And all of this happens in a way that builds symptoms of addiction: an inability to quit, withdrawal symptoms if they do, and a constant urge to feel endorphins fed by mindlessly scrolling. These addictive qualities are especially frightening because research is beginning to show heavy social media use is leading to changes in not only *how* the brain works but even the *size* and other physical qualities of the brain in ways that may be causing young people to be even more likely to focus on getting superficial approval from their peers and even less on self-control. It seems to us like a frankly terrifying self-perpetuating loop when looking at the research because it means social media companies are essentially profiting off of changing the ways young people's brains develop to make them even more likely to crave and depend on social media in the future.

Psychologists, policymakers, parents, and teachers are not the only ones torn between concern about the ways that internet-based technologies are affecting young people and hope for their potential—young people are as well. Though we did not come to interviews with questions about the role tech plays in student engagement, a number of interviewees spoke about both benefits and downsides they had experienced with a wider range of these technologies than what Prinstein addresses. Many of these stories were prompted by the relative recency of coming out of pandemic-based school use of technology; young people discussed the effects of Zoom and remote or hybrid learning on their ability to engage in school. Though we (hopefully) won't encounter lockdown-driven tech use in high schools and colleges again sometime soon, these stories are still worth learning from because they can help us spot where the lingering negative effects of pandemic-induced increased tech are still occurring and where positive effects have been lost in the return to "normal." While Zoom fatigue and other problems introduced specifically by suddenly having school online may no longer be an issue we need to worry about solving, mindful use of technology in education remains a relevant topic, especially because so many schools retained much higher usage of in-school technology after the lockdowns ended than they had before COVID-19.

Media Oversaturation

Caprielle: "We're so used to seeing so much media that I don't think older generations, or we ourselves, truly understand the detriments."

When we asked Caprielle our standard closing question, "What is one thing that you would want an adult to know about this generation?" she honed in on the effects of technological differences:

I think it's an obvious fact that [we] grew up with smartphones and technology, and yes, I can probably work the interface of Snapchat and Instagram better than my grandma, of course. But I don't think the older generations understand the repercussions of growing up in that environment, surrounded by technology, in terms of mental illness and struggles. [Like] body dysmorphia, and anxiety and depression, and seeing things that you shouldn't have seen, and PTSD. . . . Not to mention how . . . we've literally seen war footage, people dying of the pandemic, economic crises, and false news. And we're just so used to seeing so much mass media that I don't think the older generations, or we truly ourselves, understand the detriments of it. So, I think that's just a big thing of how we're struggling with a whole new face of struggles than older generations have. They've just missed that stage.

Caprielle's emphasis on the negative mental health effects is squarely matched by the research Prinstein cited to Congress, and concern about adolescent mental health was indeed why he'd been called to address Congress in the first place.

Caprielle goes on to give specific examples of ways she's seen the social approval that young people are naturally seeking get distorted by the technological platforms that need goes through. For example, she talks about how she or her peers "see teenagers that they wish they looked like, that they wouldn't see in person, or like where it's photoshopped or something," and it adds to the issues with body dysmorphia in ways that couldn't happen so readily otherwise. This perception is also supported by the research Dr. Prinstein shared that exposure to comparisons of "appearance, friends, and social activities" on social media "is associated with lower self-image and distorted body perceptions among young people."[57]

Caprielle also noted how young people seem to be experimenting with dangerous activities younger than before:

I've definitely been around people where they prioritize social life, or what they look like, or fitting in, in terms of doing drugs or . . . going along with the crowd more than academics. I definitely looked at it from an observer's eye, where I was like, "Oh my god, what are you all doing? We have a test on Monday." And [I] never came from a judgmental point of view because it's just the society that we grow up in, and we're just so accustomed to seeing it: people dating at a younger age, or just doing things at a younger age than what it used to be. We're progressively decreasing the age for certain things. I think that social media, or just media in general, has a lot to do with that.[58]

Again, Caprielle's hypothesis that social media plays a role in this change was substantiated by the research shared by

Prinstein, which showed that social media heightens the risk for peer influence to spark "illegal, immoral, dangerous, and unethical behavior.[59] because the presence of "likes" on posts of risky behavior dampen the initial inhibitions young people had about that kind of behavior: If someone just sees a picture of someone doing something stupid, they're likely to think "that's stupid" and not do it—but if they see that same picture with a bunch of likes on it, they're much less likely to think that. This tendency, combined with the tendency of people to "like" things others have liked, which in turn predicts what kinds of posts the algorithms in social media feed to the user, can make increasingly risky or unethical behavior seem more and more normal because teens see more and more posts about it, with the "likes" implying lots of their peers think that behavior is not only normal, but cool, funny, or interesting.

Caprielle also, in general, felt that various distortions in the media make it harder to "expect nothing and appreciate everything," which was her main advice to younger students. As she put it, "I think expectations are the first step to disappointment. . . . Having any expectations is the best way to be disappointed in absolutely anything, especially experiences. So, I just want to emphasize that the *High School Musical* Disney Channel media . . . that you were promised . . . you're gonna be disappointed and not get that." Caprielle felt that she and her peers would have been much better off if their expectations of high school were more aligned with reality.

King: "We had to take a break [from] social media."

King and his family noticed that the effects of social media were so harmful that they needed to drop it entirely. In his case, it was specifically seeing, as part of the surge in discussions of racism following the murder of George Floyd, "people joking about this stuff. And seeing it on social media, we had to take a break [from] social media. . . . I haven't touched social media since 2020. And I don't want to touch social media because I know that if I do, I'm going to get caught up in stuff that I don't need to be getting caught up with." For King, this break wasn't about stepping away from engaging in the issues he cared about but, instead, a way to focus that energy on his local community, where his engagement had a better overall positive effect on his well-being rather than the negative one that getting sucked into cruel or dismissive discussions online had.

King's individual experience is echoed by the research summary Prinstein shared with Congress, which showed that discrimination and cyberbullying are both more vicious online than in person, often specifically targeting young people who are part of "racial, ethnic, gender, and sexual minorities," and are significantly more likely to increase the risk for depression and anxiety than the effects of similarly discriminatory behavior experienced offline. Furthermore, Grace has also noticed that with the current trends in media, there is a more specific pressure to be not only generally well-informed but continuously up to speed with a 24-hour news cycle:

> *It's common for young people to feel pressure to be socially aware and up to date with the constantly changing social discourse and news, which will continue to be featured either on our For You pages or [at] the top of our Instagram reels. This may be part of the reason why social activists are common on social media, because social media is where many young people are getting their news. Unfortunately, it's also the reason why if some people take a break from social media, there's some level of guilt about falling short on being "socially aware" and "politically correct." The constant scrolling takes up a lot of time and attention, and it can turn into "doom scrolling," which has a significantly negative impact on our mental health.*

This is what King was experiencing, and it makes sense that it required such a conscious choice to take a step back.

The Internet Has Both Helped and Hindered Students' Education

Some interviewees spoke more directly about the various positive and negative effects technology had on their education, especially the increased use of technology prompted by online schooling during the pandemic. On the one hand, it created more freedom and choice than is possible otherwise. On the other hand, it could be distracting or disengaging, making it harder to learn and easier to cheat. One student, Connor, also pointed out how the effects of school responses to the coronavirus accelerated more haphazard use of technology in education, even after students returned to in-person school.

Vivian: "It was easier to get involved . . . because it was so accessible."

For Vivian, going online for lockdown meant she could participate in clubs and activities from home, which freed her up to join far more extracurriculars than she had been able to do in person:

> I actually didn't do any clubs [in my] freshman year; I only did sports. So, sophomore year, when [we were] fully virtual, that was the year that I got the most involved in extracurriculars. . . . Which seems counterintuitive, but for me, it was easier to get involved and really be engaged because it was so accessible to just be able to join Zoom meetings. . . . I would say for most students,

virtual school had the opposite effect. Because virtual school, for most people, was really, really tough. But personally, for me, it was so much easier to manage my time. Because I didn't have to factor in transportation time. It was so easy for me just to click, click, and click. And I'm also in a household that is quiet all the time. So it's easy for me to focus.

Vivian was obviously conscious of the differences between her experience and that of many other students, but her story is not entirely unusual. It connects to experiences we've discussed already, like Eddie, who was able to get all his requirements out of the way his junior year primarily because of the flexibility and lack of social distractions virtual school provided, and King, whose virtual homeschool curriculum allowed him to make his local library a second home, or Caprielle, who felt free to pursue academic success because of being able to focus exclusively on classes, with no distractions, in her online dual-enrolled program.

Obviously, some of these examples no longer apply; most schools removed online-based options as vaccines became widely available for students and teachers and because in-person school is better for most students. However, Vivian's story illustrates an inadvertent benefit that is lost when students have to factor in transportation as part of the equation for participating in extracurriculars, perhaps indicating that there could be some benefits to schools offering some clubs and activities that can be accessed online for those students who can't otherwise participate, especially since meaningful extracurricular choices can provide a significant boost to feeling engaged in school.

Zimo: "Not having your phones [was] . . . a necessary and useful thing."

Zimo, on the other hand, talked about how distracting technology can be, including when in person in the classroom:

> *I know this is something that should not have been an issue, if I go around self-proclaiming as an undergraduate student, but their policies on computers and phones . . . impact things substantially. Because I'll be honest, for the Fall '21 classes, I myself spent a fair chunk of time around screens instead of giving any amount of attention to what's going on in that class, but for the Spring '22 [semester], we were expected to just be in the discussion, by not having our phones and [tech] in use, which, I hate to admit, it's kind of a necessary and useful thing with regards to increasing engagement in class.*

He felt bad about succumbing to tech distractions, especially because he felt like it undermined him thinking of himself as an undergraduate student rather than a high-schooler (he shared this story in the context of his dual-enrolled program). But his honesty is refreshing, and while he may be looking at it as a shortcoming of his age, it could also just be seen as relatively universal for most humans: if anyone has a device in their eye-line that has access to infinite information and entertainment, are they really going to find it easy to focus? Research at UT Austin, for example, shows that even having a phone near enough to reach, even if notifications are turned off, decreases the brain's ability to perform a cognitive task because some unconscious or conscious mental energy is spent on controlling the urge to check one's phone.[60] Zimo's story expands the potential implications of this study since he points out that having his computer open during class was just as distracting, even if it made it easier to take notes, because it offered the temptation of checking on or viewing other things that had nothing to do with class.

————————————————

Melanie: "It's difficult to pay attention on a screen."

Melanie also talked about how distracting easy tech access was for her. Though in her case, it was in relation to virtual school during COVID-19 precautions, it has implications for post-COVID-19 classroom tech use as well:

> *It was so hard to learn online. Because there's just so many distractions. You get so tired sitting in the chair; I would lay in my bed sometimes, and I'd fall asleep. . . . When teachers were playing videos, that was awful, because I would just fall asleep or go on my phone, go on TikTok, go on whatever.*

For Melanie, it was not just the distraction of tech but also the disconnectedness of it that made virtual schooling difficult, making her eager to return to in-person school as quickly as possible. She put it succinctly: "It's difficult to pay attention on a screen. Especially when your peers also aren't interested. . . . Most people didn't have their cameras on, like sometimes I was the only one with my camera on because . . . I hoped [teachers] would like me more if I had my camera on."

As we discussed in the chapter on teachers, she, therefore, especially appreciated it when one teacher held open "office hours" rather than just the "recorded lectures" that "most teachers did," because "a couple of my friends and I would just hop on and talk not just about chemistry. We caught up on life. . . . I am a very social person, and meeting to talk was so important." In her description of how most teachers approached virtual school, we also get hints of some of the factors that might explain why online learning could be empowering for some and disengaging for others: if the online environment was just asynchronous content consumption, with no interaction, who wouldn't prefer watching something that was designed to be entertaining instead?

Of course, it's no surprise that teachers who are suddenly asked to engage in virtual instruction when they've never had to before would struggle to do it in the "best" way:

Some of the teachers that I had heard about for years, that were [supposed to be] "the best teacher you'll ever have," they were not great over Google Meet, not super engaging. It's really hard for them, I think, to engage students, especially when students are cheating, students are not turning their cameras on, [or] not turning in their assignments. And there's just a kind of energy of sitting in front of a screen, not being able to talk to your friends, even [when we were back] in school, being six feet apart from your friends, not really being able to interact the same way. It's really hard. I felt very lucky in the classes that I had friends in; we would just text, right? Maybe not the most academically studious thing to do, but it definitely made the class better.

Overall, Melanie found that the online versions of classes were "lower quality than [she] would have hoped for," which she found disappointing in electives she'd been looking forward to for years.

This lower quality, prompted by difficulties adapting to the online teaching environment, also made less interesting required courses even harder than they already would have been and made cheating both easier and more desirable. "My math class was bad with that; he was not great with technology, [and] his lecturing was really boring. Not great at teaching; nice guy, but not great at teaching. His grades were inconsistent, [and] cheating was a big issue." As Melanie put it at another point, "cheating is a different issue within COVID and non-COVID," and this was primarily due to the online environment.

While everything that Melanie describes may just seem like a list of the reasons it's a good thing school moved back to the physical classroom, the effects she describes of learning online are still worth keeping in mind as we rely on more and more technology within the classroom. When students are placed on laptops or tablets in class to complete assignments, it can be an opportunity for students to learn and work at their own pace—but it can also be an opportunity to space out and disconnect, checking what interesting websites haven't been blocked by the school's internet server yet (for instance, my middle-school-aged son comes home with a new one the school hasn't found out about yet that "all the kids are using" about once a month or so). Additionally, if this is done instead of activities that increase students' sense of belonging and connection with their teachers and peers, it could still serve to decrease overall school engagement, even (perhaps especially) if they seem to love the school-sanctioned screen time.

Connor: "Technology is not being used to deliberately improve the classroom."

Like Melanie, Connor also noticed how the particular ways of using tech sparked by COVID-19 led to more cheating and disengagement:

> *Things like Zoom have made it easier to cheat or to kind of skip out on class. I know people who do that. I understand why students do that; when you're stressed about grades, [you do] anything you can do to get ahead because post-secondary admissions and college applications sucks. [But doing things online] allows for more of a lack of empathy, [more] cheating, more disengagement, just because it's almost like there's a wall because being in your home is different than being in the classroom and*

learning because your home is kind of your life space, and . . . it's good to have that separation physically; it's helpful for a lot of students, but there's a lot of factors that go into that.

Unlike Melanie, however, Connor also raised concerns about the long-term implications of how technological access and use unfolded during the pandemic. First, he spoke about the effects of the digital divide, which he still saw persisting even after regional efforts to provide internet and devices to students:

I gotta speak from Kentucky's perspective here; there's a very real digital divide. I know people who aren't online, who don't have a way to be online, so with the way COVID was affecting school, they didn't have a way to plug in, so it really affected them because you just can't learn in that environment; it's really difficult. And then others I know, if they do have access to the internet, it isn't great, and their technology isn't great; it tends to be pretty old and slow and can't even support things like Zoom, so it makes it very challenging for students. Things have gotten a little better [since 2020], but we still have a real divide.

The effects of this divide compound the effects of COVID-19 learning loss, and that learning loss has already been discussed in the national news *ad nauseam*, so we won't rehash it here.

However, Connor shared that "for those who do have access to technology, it feels like it's replacing school—like you could ask a lot of high school students, and a good number of them would probably say that they learned more from TikTok and Twitter than they did from school. There's something to be said for that!" This matches a phenomenon we've now heard anecdotally from several high school teachers: they have students who inform them that since they could learn any subject from a more interesting video online, they see no reason they should bother listening in class if they're bored. It's a difficult argument to respond to since the general point of public education—that not everyone has that access, but everyone has a right to education—does nothing to change the point those students are making about their individual learning. This effect also makes the issue of a digital divide a more insidious problem because it means students with more resources now have yet another way to get better learning while giving the illusion that tech access disparities are resolved by having students in the same building.

In turn, the often-sizable gap between how the students with the greatest tech access can comfortably navigate even new technology versus how their own teachers navigate new tech can create even more obstacles. Connor talked about this as well:

> *Even today, watching teachers struggle with tech is kind of a constant . . . things like in-class quizzes or different tech things, and it is really, really difficult [watching that]. I could get into a rant here about the privatization of education through technology. . . . But I think, ultimately, technology is less something that augments and improves education and more something that replaces and, at times, hinders it; sometimes, having technology gives more of a barrier to access to education than not having it in the first place.*

For someone as invested in student voice as Connor is, who also is pursuing a technology-related career, we can only imagine just how "really, really difficult" it was to watch teachers fumble with something that could have been done both with greater technical proficiency and with more rewarding autonomy if students had instead been at the helm of that tech use.

Connor went on to get into the details of what he meant

about technology being both a help and a hindrance in educational settings:

> There's a lot that's hard to disentangle there because technology does have a lot of pros in education: having access to things in collaborative Google Docs, being able to make slides really easily is great, you have a better sense of engineering, and it's easier for students to engage with something they otherwise wouldn't have. [That's] all really useful, but at times, there might be an overapplication of technology. . . . It feels like there are a lot of teachers who feel obligated to do tech, but technology doesn't necessarily help anything; students aren't more engaged, [and] they aren't more tuned into their education because of technology. I don't think it helps that; if anything, it puts a hindrance on it, even for the good things technology does, where just having it available . . . can be a way to disengage from education, to replace education, for better or worse. No one has really figured out a way to solve for that.

Connor summed up his general take by saying that "it feels like we're just letting technology . . . shift [education] away from paper and pencil to more digital, but it's not radically transforming what education looks like; it's not being used to deliberately improve the classroom."

Digitizing classrooms and educational methods that weren't previously engaging isn't going to suddenly make them engaging—and, in the meantime, young people are offered more and more attention-grabbing alternatives from the internet that make the classroom dynamics even more stilted in comparison. These effects aren't going away in the wake of the pandemic; if anything, as advancements in AI seem to storm the news almost weekly these days (as we write these words in 2023), it has become an even more pressing issue to actually listen to students about how their voluntary and school-sponsored encounters with internet-based tech are helping and hindering their ability and interest to learn.

What to Do About Screens' Effects on Student Motivation

Deciding how and where to get involved in an adolescent's exposure to, and use of, internet-based tech is an incredibly thorny issue. We've heard from parents who say they wish they'd never given smartphones to their kids in the first place because it became so hard to close that particular Pandora's box once it was opened. These parents hate the effects of phone use, especially social media use, that they see unfolding on their kids but feel powerless to pull them out of it because so many teens use this as their means of communication—and many school extracurriculars use social media platforms to connect group participants and communicate about their activities. We've also heard from parents who say their kids are perfectly fine and measured in how they use the internet and social media and that they've seen no issues arise from having access. There is no simple solution or single right way to approach the role of internet-based tech inside education or young people's lives in general.

However, in the introduction to this chapter, we deliberately quoted the exact language of "exploit" and "capitalize" from Prinstein. Those words imply what's worth stating directly: large companies are making significant profits off of playing to the vulnerabilities inherent in how human brains develop. While Prinstein was addressing Congress to talk about what policy changes and regulations that vulnerability should spark, young people and the adults who care about them don't have to wait for that systemic level of change to occur (though policy-level changes are certainly worth advocating for). For adults who are looking for how to bring these risks to young people's attention, it's worth following the guidance laid out by Brian Galla, an associate professor of applied developmental psychology, in "Rebel With a Cause: Help Teens Resist the Pull of Social Media."[61] He found young people were more likely to express interest in changing their social media use when they were shown the kind of "social-media trickery" used by businesses to increase their profit than when they were shown information about how bad social media was for their brains and overall well-being. He explains the details of how the effective approach was framed in the short blog post with that title, so we recommend reading it in full. It's also worth reading a short Q&A with Prinstein on the APA's website, where he discusses specific strategies parents can use to build their kids' resistance to the negative effects of social media. He recommends these conversations start before kids get on social media and that the conversations continue periodically after they are on it.[62]

The other big screen time activity that can affect teens' overall motivation, and academic motivation specifically, is excessive video game use. For example, online game addiction was found to decrease Chinese college students' overall academic motivation, but higher levels of academic engagement were found to mediate this effect.[63] As with social media use, there are unhealthy and healthy ways of gaming, and while the former can have detrimental effects, the latter can actually support motivation (for example, some students can successfully leverage gaming enjoyment as a reward system for unmotivating homework tasks, like allowing ten minutes of game time for every 30 minutes of homework completed). As with any other screen time use, the trick is to keep the lines of communication open and have boundaries in place that make it more likely your teen is building healthy habits than unhealthy ones.

For adults working within educational settings, it's also worth considering whether you can use the information shared here to spark collaboration with young people who are bothered by what they see, as some of our interviewees were, to advocate for change to school practices around tech. Together, students and school staff could decide what kind of classroom policies would work best around technology and whether there are opportunities for student-led teacher professional development on how to use technology in ways that make school more engaging. There's an opportunity to both enhance student voice and improve everyone's learning if we don't continue to make it yet another thing teachers are supposed to take the lead on learning. If you want some inspiration from a young person who took the lead in her community, specifically around smartphones and social media, check out an interview with Logan Lane, student founder of the "Luddite Club" in Brooklyn.[64] Or you can just go directly to the young people you know and engage them in a conversation about all the ways tech and the internet are being used during their day and what effects they see it having on them and their peers. The fact that our interviewees offered this much insight about tech effects when we never asked questions directly about technology is telling: young people are thinking about tech, they're noticing its effects, and at least some of them would be interested in taking action if they saw they'd get support doing it.

More Ideas From Experienced Practitioners

Remember that many tech companies are hiring some of the best psychologists to manipulate us into using technology more than we intended. They are using a deep understanding of human behavior, reward responses, and neurobiology to entice us to use more technology than we intended. There are a few techniques that may help counteract the psychological manipulation:

1. Parents need to provide a good example of limiting technology and using it conscientiously. Then, parents and

children should set rules for the overall use of technology together. These rules are bi-directional in that children can help parents if they notice parents' distractibility or overuse of technology. Just like when learning to drive, we don't send teenagers off into the wild without extensive practice and instruction, so do we give instruction and oversight of technology. We also provide them with positive examples when learning to drive and expect them to follow suit, so parents also need to clean up their acts around the use of technology.

2. Use the screen-tracking features in your tech. Most smartphones can track how much time you are spending on them. Check this occasionally to get a real picture of your usage and if you feel like it is too much or in an appropriate range. Ask yourself, "Do I agree to being manipulated in this way?" if you find you are overusing a specific app and the answer is "no," please delete or otherwise modify apps that you feel you are overusing.

3. Turn off or mute as many notifications as possible. The constant buzzing, chiming, and alerts are key psychological hooks to lure you back in.

4. If you are finding yourself staying up too late, ask yourself, "Would I actually wake up 30 minutes early to do this?" If the answer is "yes," for example, catching up with a close friend or relative in a different time zone, then keep doing it. If the answer is "no way," then it's not worth your time and you are being manipulated into its use.

5. Watch for if you are "revenge procrastinating" using technology. Many people feel that they have spent their entire day doing what others tell them to do, and then will try to reward themselves later with times to goof off playing video games or using other technology. The important

thing here is to act with intention rather than acting by default over the activity that is easiest to access. If you find yourself revenge procrastinating, ask yourself these questions: "Is this actually what I want to do with my time?" and "Am I hurting myself or am I filling myself up?" and most importantly, "What are some truly fun things that I have to look forward to?"

Remember also that technology is not without its value, including allowing wonderfully close connections with people who are far away, enriching our knowledge base, allowing access to experts that were otherwise inaccessible, and allowing wonderful works of creativity, collaboration, and exploration. If you're confident your screen use at home or in the classroom is doing this, then don't worry about it.

8

Final Thoughts

When that student wrote, "Can you help me give a shit about high school? I want to, but I just don't know how," on her class worksheet, she captured a sentiment that was immediately recognizable to every student we spoke with. For some, the hope of college was enough to make it easier to engage in their learning, but that wasn't a guarantee. Simply biding time, as if high school is just an especially long and painful waiting room to survive, writes off four years of opportunity. It also makes it harder to thrive in college because teens haven't developed the skills and mindsets to make the most of the greater autonomy college allows. It's almost impossible to sustain motivation to learn in environments that do not set students up to recognize and build on relevant abilities, to help them experience a sense of belonging and connection, and to support them in making meaningful choices. It takes a collaborative effort by parents, educators, and young people themselves to change environments like these. The need to collaborate only increases if there are extra barriers, like unwelcoming communities, high-pressure environments, or addictive technologies warring for a young person's attention.

None of this is new information. Researchers have studied all the elements of positive youth development, effective education, and motivation for decades. What is missing is public awareness and the will to do something about it on both large and small scales. What's also missing, far too often, is the willingness to put young people at the center of creating their own change. Adolescence is an incredibly potent time of development and energy that is too often wasted. We hope this book sparks ideas on ways to change that. If adults can shift their relationships with teens to connect first and then become their co-pilots in exploration, trial-and-error, and decision-making, then school has the potential to become not only engaging as it happens but also successful at setting up young people to continue to learn and navigate the unknown as they enter adulthood.

Working *with*, rather than *on* or *for*, young people is crucial for several reasons. Variations of the call "nothing about us without us" have been utilized for centuries by marginalized groups to advocate to those who held decision-making power[65] because any other approach is ineffective, unfair, and dehumanizing. Any initiative is more likely to succeed if it's been co-created with everyone involved. Additionally, the very act of getting involved and seeing where their decisions are actually making a difference, in and of itself, makes school more engaging for teens. It also gives them the opportunity to develop crucial skills they'll need throughout their adult lives: perspective-taking, critical thought, teamwork, planning, and so on.

If you've read this book, chances are it's because you care deeply about teens and are willing to devote some of your time and energy to help them. But it's also likely you've got a dozen demands competing for your attention: adulting is hard, and parenting (or working in schools) is even harder. At a time when parents are fried by worry and competing demands for their attention and when educators' burnout levels are at record highs,[66] giving teens more agency is not only vital for young people's success; it's the only sustainable path forward for adults, too.

We don't offer this recommendation naively. It's not the equivalent of taking a snooze in the back while someone else takes the wheel; it's real work for adults and teens to collaborate this way, especially when we're first negotiating how to make it happen. If just the thought of that feels too exhausting to consider right now, don't feel guilty, and know you're not alone. For example, I still haven't dredged up the energy to sit down with my middle schooler and find out what kind of publicly available high school options we have in our district. It's hard to figure out where that fits between work, meal prep, household chores, and the everyday stressors and joys of family life. To combat my worry and guilt, I remind myself that I can always focus on the most important thing without having to find more time in my day to do it: our relationship. I try to build that relationship weekly by listening to my kids without an agenda, sharing my enthusiasm for the things I'm passionate about, and being genuinely interested in their passions. I also try to involve them in problem-solving whenever the opportunity comes up (even though I sometimes find it hard not to just tell them how to fix it). I remind myself daily that *how* I show up with them is more important than *how many* things we do and that, like in any marathon, I need to pace myself if I want to make it to the finish line.

Similar principles hold for young people, who may sometimes feel buried under a different onslaught of pressures: social dynamics (in person and online), questions of who they are and what they want, worries about both the present and the future, and for some, a mountain of homework, test-prep, and college-applications. Finding the time and energy to seek out better relationships, advocate for meaningful choices, and build confidence in their ability to learn can feel like monumental tasks. Trying to tackle them all at once would likely be daunting enough to make even the biggest overachievers turn apathetic just to protect themselves. For example, even after writing this book, Grace shared:

I am still continuously finding ways to build my motivation when I'm overwhelmed and dejected. When I started to build skills that helped me feel a level of autonomy, it felt scary, especially because I didn't feel like I had been afforded the opportunity to explore my independence and make those meaningful choices. But when I made the time to explore my interests and build my confidence inside and outside of school, I felt more whole, like my identity was more than just my education. I found myself building skills that allowed me to feel more competent (like baking), making plans with my friends, driving, prioritizing knowing myself through therapy, journaling, and going on walks—all of which feel like meaningful choices. Ultimately, it encouraged me to be more motivated to show up for myself in more ways than one.

Building and sustaining motivation is not just a one-and-done thing; it's an ongoing process.

It may help both young people and adults to think of building up abilities, belonging, and choices as a switchback road up a steep mountain. If we start small with enjoyable ways of creating connections, we build up enough trust to consider a new choice or ability we hadn't been willing to try before. We go higher as we begin to see success, and the road doubles back over itself: strengthening relationships, gaining more confidence, finding bigger choices we care about, and acting on them. We form new goals and find it energizes us to pursue them. That's the beauty of investing in building sustainable motivation—as we do so, we get more energy rather than less.

That's not to say it's a perfect formula; everyone has their moments where pursuing a goal doesn't feel nearly as appealing as binge-watching a favorite show. Lasting motivation is more of a road trip than back-to-back jet flights, and thank goodness—detours and rest stops are far more manageable over the long haul than high-speed forces that fly past everything in their path. But when you find yourself with more of an empty tank than usual, check in on whether you feel like you have the abilities, belonging, and choices that matter to you. Doing so not only helps you spot what you need to do to regain your own momentum, but it also helps you model this process of reflection and realignment to young people you care about. It also helps you empathize with teens who are struggling to find their own way to sustain a desire to learn or with other parents and educators who feel worried, overwhelmed, and burned out.

Whether you're an educator or a parent, we hope this book makes it easier to experience that empathy for teens, parents, and educators, as it's a powerful way to build a sense of connection that can begin to refuel everyone's motivation. The greatest gift you can give teens is your willingness to listen deeply and collaborate openly. Luckily, that gift comes with its own rewards: insight, curiosity, and the excitement of seeing someone learn and grow in ways you never could have imagined if you'd remained behind the wheel.

Resources

For a living list of resources for parents, educators, and young people, see www.BeccaBlock.com/resources. We included a few here you might want to use right away.

TL;DR: Take-Away Tips

1. **Connect first and last.** Neither you nor the teens you care about will be able to build lasting motivation without good relationships.

2. **Be a model.** Diagnose your own motivation to build up your energy and model it for teens. (See the next resource for help with this).

3. **Help them take the wheel**—but don't leave the car just yet! Teens need to scaffold into adulthood. That means they need to exercise their growing abilities to make real choices and experience the real results, good and bad, of those choices while still getting the support they need to feel confident.

4. **Remember that relevance can happen in a range of ways.** Long-term goals, hands-on activities, connecting to interests, and challenging teens to think deeply about meaningful topics are always to make learning feel more relevant.

5. **Think carefully about when and how to use external rewards.** External rewards, like praise, money, food, or screen time, can be effective for short-term bursts of motivation to plow through boring but necessary tasks. However, overusing them not only erodes their effectiveness; it also

can block people from developing more internal sources of reward, like pride in helping someone, in a hard job well done, or in making progress toward a meaningful goal.

6. **Explore new possibilities.** Having a wide variety of experiences is far more likely to spark long-term goals than direct pressure to engage in goal setting. Break out of ruts— meet new people, do new activities, and leverage the power of boredom without easy fixes (e.g., not getting to just jump on a screen) to spark creativity and a desire to explore.

7. **Build confidence in the ability to learn.** You can help build student confidence by pointing out where they got better at something when they worked at it—but this will be ignored if it's disingenuous. Start with yourself and check where you've inadvertently reinforced ideas that talent is fixed rather than learned.

8. **Talk about the effects of screens** (especially gaming and social media) early and often. Engage teens' inclination to rebel by pulling back the curtain on the ways companies use psychology to hook and manipulate people so they can make more money. Model auditing your own screen use so teens' sensitivity to hypocrisy isn't triggered.

TL;DR: Learning Your ABCs

Abilities: Are you feeling capable of doing or learning the skills you need to be successful? Do those skills feel relevant to you? If not, try to:

- Identify where you feel stuck: is it because you think you can't get good at something or because you don't see why you should try? Honestly interrogate yourself on this because one of these can often serve as cover for the other (apathy is a great protection against trying hard and failing).

- Look for where you got better at something similar. What did you do? What helped you keep trying over time? Learning from your own comparable experiences can help more than following someone else's blueprint.

- Dig for the relevance of the skill you're struggling with. Where else might it help you, now or later? Are there hobbies or careers that leverage this skill that you may want to have open to you later in life?

Belonging: Do you feel connected to the people around you? Do they care about both you and what you're trying to accomplish? If not, try to:

- Have more open conversations. Seems simple, but getting to know people is the only way to begin connecting with them. Ask people about what they love to do, their favorite foods, and the famous people they'd most love to meet. If you're looking to spark more conversations as a family, get a box of questions to keep at the dining room table and grab them to spark ideas for dinner conversation beyond "How was your day?"

- Check your existing relationships. What isn't working yet? If you don't have relationships in the context where you lack motivation (e.g., you don't particularly know any of your coworkers), challenge yourself to ask one personable question a day to start to build those relationships. If you have relationships but don't feel supported in what you're trying to accomplish, investigate why. Often, it's as simple as communicating to people what we're trying to do, and once we do, they're happy to support us.

- Avoid the superficial hits of connection brought on by "likes" and "shares." These have been designed to feed into our need for social connection and approval, but they're like candy: they'll fill you up for the moment but leave you hungry and feeling bad again a little while later.

Choices: What choices do you have right now? Do they feel like they matter? If not, try to:

- Reflect on how you're thinking about your options. Can you analyze the things you "have to" do to find where you're actually making a choice because there's something you want?[67]

- Find new choices. Where have you been assuming there are no other options but haven't fully investigated to make sure you're right? Where it relates to school, this can look like assuming there are no useful classes, no enjoyable extracurriculars, or no meaningful and affordable alternatives to the public high school itself.

- Ask a friend for help. It's often hard to spot the ruts we're in and what we might be overlooking, but the people around us will find them easier to spot (just like you can probably more easily think of a handful of ways your friends aren't noticing choices they have).

The Interviewees

We offer brief descriptions here of the interviewees we directly quoted throughout the book, alphabetized by first name so that you can quickly page here in the midst of reading if you want to remind yourself of the details about someone as you read what they said. We had the good fortune of being able to talk to dozens of young people between the ages of 15-22 from across the United States during the first half of 2022, and 19 of them have stories we share in this book. As mentioned in the Authors' Note, most names here are pseudonyms. There are more details about some than others because we based our descriptions on whatever details each young person wanted to share about themselves.[68]

Ava (Asian, 17, she/her), at the time of our interview, was a senior in high school in the Southeast. She described where she lived as rural, and she planned to go to a university in her home state but was looking forward to the larger population and more diverse views she would encounter there. She had attended both private and public schools, including, briefly, a boarding school before COVID lockdown sent her back home. When we asked how she wanted to be described, she also shared, "I have four siblings. I'm the second oldest. My mom and dad are first-generation immigrants, so I'm a second-generation immigrant from Vietnam. I paint, and I'm third in the class at my school. I'm in many organizations. I'm Catholic [and] a first-generation college student, and I'll be attending [a well-known university in her state] in the fall." Ava did see herself as a high-performing student.

Ariya (Black and Puerto Rican, 18, she/her), at the time of our interview, was also a senior in high school. She had attended public schools throughout K-12 in a different state in the Southeast and was in a fairly populous urban-suburban town. She considered herself to be a high-performing student and kept a very full schedule to stay competitive for college admissions. Getting into a competitive college was important to her career plans.

Avery (Asian and White, 16, he/him), at the time of our interview, was a junior in high school in a highly populated suburban school district in the mid-Atlantic region. Both his parents were also teachers in that same public school district. He did not identify as a particularly high-performing or low-performing student and did not have specific college or career goals in mind when we spoke with him.

Brian (Asian and White, 19, he/him), at the time of our interview, had recently completed his high school diploma via an alternative home-schooling program. He had not yet decided if he wanted to go to college and described how he had recently been diagnosed as being on the autism spectrum. Up until his final two years of high school, he had attended public schools in a highly populated suburban school district in the mid-Atlantic region. He saw himself as someone who had generally struggled in school and who wasn't interested in academic performance, though he did like learning in specific subject areas that interested him.

Caprielle (White, 17, she/her), at the time of our interview, was dual enrolled as both a junior in high school and a first year in her local community college in a suburban area in the Northwest. Academic achievement was very important to her and her family; she described her household as very female-empowerment-oriented about education. Coming from a divorced family, she was raised solely by her single mother and two older sisters.

Connor (White, 18, he/him), at the time of our interview, was dual-enrolled as both a high-school senior and a second-year in an on-campus dual-enrollment program for high-achieving STEM students in a rural part of the Midwest. Neither of his parents has a college degree, but both are very supportive of his education. He was also very active in student voice efforts in his state, and when we asked him to describe himself, he said, "I'm a White man, I'm gay, I'm cis, I come from the Cincinnati area, I'm a Kentuckian, I'm a scientist, [and] I'm a researcher in computer science, bioinformatics, and sociology; I want to improve communities. I want to find a way to use technology for good and to solve problems the world is facing both between global and local levels." He also laughed and said, "I might add as an addendum to that description, 'some of that may change.'" We left in his identifying details because Connor felt he'd already been so active in fairly public student voice efforts in Kentucky that anonymizing his profile would be pointless.

Eddie (Black, 18, he/him), at the time of our interview, had just finished his senior year of high school in a public school in the suburban Northwest that had access to an unusual trade school and some other alternative programs. He was a football player and fairly popular, but didn't like the social dynamics of high school. He was planning on attending college the following semester and was interested in becoming a computer programmer. He didn't see himself as a particularly high- or low-achieving student.

Elena (Asian, 18, she/her or they/them), at the time of our interview, was finishing up her senior year at a public high school in the Southeast. She was passionate about art and planned to attend college to major in an art-related area. Academic achievement was somewhat important to her, but she did not experience some of the same pressures for academic performance that she saw in her peers.

Goose (Latina, 17, she/her), at the time of our interview, had just finished her senior year in a public high school in a suburban school district in the Northeast. She described the school district as fairly wealthy and said she'd often felt out of place having two immigrant parents from South America who didn't have the kind of high-income jobs many of her peers' parents had. She described herself as "eccentric" and as someone who was a bit "goth" and had niche interests; she also talked about how she struggled sometimes with depression and anxiety.

Grace (Asian and Black, 18, she/her), at the time of our initial interview, was in her first year at a competitive university in the mid-Atlantic. Prior to that, she had been a student at a dense suburban public high school in a different part of the mid-Atlantic. As coauthor, she continued working on this book through her second year of university. Some of the stories she includes range from all three of these time periods. Grace's parents are immigrants from Barbados and South Vietnam (father and mother, respectively). She is the youngest of four kids, each from a different generation. For more about her, see "About the Authors" at the end of the book.

Ian (Black, 16, he/him), at the time of our interview, was a junior in a vo-tech high school in the Northeast. He described himself as an animal lover, environmentalist, and a DEI advocate, and he had applied to the public vocational-technical high school because it had the opportunity to get hands-on experience that would help him discern if he wanted to be a veterinarian or a marine biologist, his two top career interests.

As we spoke, we were interrupted a few times by the various pets he cared for in his home. Ian is a kind of Renaissance student—he said his most enjoyable classes were in global studies and English because he liked the "open-ended assignments," but he's also skilled in math. He already knew multiplication and division before entering first grade, and in one of his elementary grades, he got the highest math score on the statewide test for that grade.[69]

King (Black, 15, he/him), at the time of our interview, was in an online homeschooling program as a high school freshman. Prior to that, he had been in public school from kindergarten through middle school in the Northeast, in a district that he described as predominantly White and fairly wealthy.

Layla (Black, 19, she/her), at the time of our interview, was finishing up her first year at a competitive university in the Northeast. She was born in the United States and attended public school for K-12; her parents are immigrants from Africa. She described herself as Muslim, bisexual, and someone who struggled sometimes with mental health issues. She had a passion for chemistry and science that had been encouraged by a wonderful teacher in high school, but she was finding it hard to maintain in the performative university setting she was in at the time we spoke.

Maria (Latina, 16, she/her), at the time of our interview, was in her junior year at a college-prep-focused charter school in the Southwest. She was appreciative of that college-prep focus and eager to attend college when she graduated. Her parents are immigrants from Central America.

Melanie (Asian, 18, she/her), at the time of our interview, had just graduated from a public high school in the Northeast. She described herself as a high-achieving student, a child of immigrant parents, and a queer woman, the latter of which she'd found difficult to be because her parents were not happy about it for religious reasons. She was interested in becoming a nurse rather than a doctor, though she knew her parents would have preferred she pursue medical school. She was the youngest sibling and had briefly lived with her older sister while her mother underwent extensive cancer treatments in a large city several hours away from where she lived.

Nina (White, 22, she/her), at the time of our interview, was in her second year at an open-access college in the Southeast. She had completed her high school diploma via homeschooling at age 17, and deliberately took time off before going to college to work and figure out what she wanted a college degree for. Her parents had moved several times as she was growing up and usually joined various homeschooling groups each time they settled in a new area, but Nina had never felt particularly connected to any of them. She was passionate about the activities she had gotten involved with at her college, including being a tutor in the writing center, a student in the cross-disciplinary honors college, and a member of several clubs. She planned to transfer to a four-year college and then to law school once she completed her associate's degree.

Tuesday (Asian and White, 18, he/him), at the time of our interview, was in his final year at a rural public high school in the inland Northwest. Tuesday described himself as a trans man, assigned female at birth, who had come out socially in high school but whose parents rejected his desire to be referred to as "he." He also described how he had struggled with mental health issues as a result of being frequently bullied and harassed in school, and he had deliberately gone inpatient for mental health care several times as a result. He looked forward to graduating high school and being able to leave his hometown and go somewhere where both his gender and biracial background wouldn't be treated as cause for scorn and cruelty.

Vivian (Asian, 16, she/her), at the time of our interview, was in her junior year at a suburban public high school in the mid-Atlantic. She described her high school as both unique for having an excellent IB program and also as a "majority-minority" school with many speakers of other languages, a school that was "low-performing" on traditional testing metrics compared to other schools in the district. She was a very involved student in extracurriculars, especially a county-wide program that allowed her to not only learn more about equity and history, but also then work with other students to create professional development for teachers on that subject.

Zimo (Asian, 18, he/him), at the time of our interview, was in his final year of high school and second year of an on-campus dual-enrollment program in the Southwest. He planned to go to another university in that same state once he graduated and deliberately took classes in his dual-enrollment program that would transfer easily to that university, where he wanted to study computer science. He had moved to the United States in middle school and attended public schools, but was frustrated that his math and science training from China was much higher than that of his peers in the U.S. when he first arrived.

Programs or Organizations That Interviewees Recommended

We share this list to condense what we heard from young people we spoke with. Except for the programs Grace herself experienced, we have no formal connection to any of these programs and aren't receiving any compensation for sharing the recommendations.

- Yale Young Global Scholars. Recommended by Caprielle.

- HOBY. International youth leadership program with chapters throughout many states in the U.S.A. Recommended by Ava and Grace.

- Kentucky Student Voice Team. Recommended by Connor.

- Leonard Davis Institute Summer Undergraduate Minority Research (SUMR) Program. Recommended by Grace.

- Matriculate. Recommended by Zimo. (Additionally, other students recommended reaching out to local private college counselors to see if they offer pro bono services to students who are the first in their families to go to college and/or from low-income homes.)

- GripTape. A nonprofit organization that provides grants of up to $500, plus access to a champion, for young people, ages 14–19, to pursue their own learning interests. Recommended by Melanie.

- Scholastic Art & Writing. Recommended by Elena, who also pointed out they have fee waivers for those who need them.

- Bow Seat Ocean Awareness Contest (International). Recommended by Elena.

- Fusion Global Academy. A private, fully virtual middle and high school that also offers one-to-one tutoring and add-on content for students who are attending school elsewhere. Brian experienced and recommended this school.

- The Portfolio Plus Program at Washington University in St. Louis (see https://samfoxschool.wustl.edu/academics/pre-college-programs/portfolio-plus). Recommended by Elena and described in some of her stories in the book.

Undoubtedly, there are many other programs besides these that young people have found helpful and empowering, but we wanted to share the ones that stood out to our interviewees.

Endnotes

1. Natanson, "These 64 Education Laws." Reinicke, "Florida Just Became." These two articles show examples of just some of the kinds of educational mandates schools have to navigate, from politically contentious "culture war" laws to less divisive mandates, like requiring financial literacy instruction, that still require significant time and effort to implement.

2. We opt to refer to Becca in the first person and Grace in the third to make it easier to distinguish between speakers, and so that Grace's stories would match those of other interviewees.

3. Deci, "A Meta-Analytic Review;" Li, "Extrinsic Motivation." The former is an academic article, the latter is a more parent-focused explanation of the topic. In general, extrinsic motivators have consistently been found to decrease intrinsic motivation. However, not all extrinsic motivation is equally damaging, and so simply orienting to a mental model that "intrinsic motivation = good" and "extrinsic motivation = bad" can not only make parenting and teaching (and motivating yourself!) more challenging, but it's also not fully accurate. There is a variety in the types of extrinsic motivation, and the more someone fully buys into the goal they are pushing towards as valuable to them, the more effective the extrinsic motivator is.

4. Ryan, "Self-Determination Theory;" Ackerman, "Self-Determination Theory." The former is an academic article, the latter a more layperson-friendly explanation.

5. Hodges, "School Engagement." Their definition: "engagement is a measurement of how involved, enthusiastic and committed one is to an organization" (np).

6. Search Institute, "The Developmental Relationships Framework." This brief web article offers insights on how young people of all ages benefit from having authentic, mutually supportive relationships with adults and what the characteristics of these kinds of relationships are.

7. Lythcott-Haims, *How to Raise an Adult.* It's not a coincidence that this was a best-selling book. It still accurately describes the trap that is hard for many parents to avoid.

8. Wallace, *Never Enough*, 1-22. The first chapter has insights into the pressures driving both public and private high schools. For more academic sources, see Ebbert, "Complexities in Adjustment Patterns" and Luthar, "High-Achieving Schools."

9. Bandura, "Human Agency." We're influenced by Albert Bandura's foundational work here, and all the psychologists who have built upon it, who have found that people are healthier and more fulfilled when they genuinely believe they have the ability to exercise control over their lives.

10. Pinquart, "Associations of Parenting Styles." This academic article documents the effect parenting styles can have on academic achievement.

11. Howard, "Student Motivation and Associated Outcomes." This meta-analysis of multiple articles shows how intrinsic motivation relates to student success and well-being, how personal value relates to persistence, and how motivation to obtain rewards or avoid punishment did not drive performance or persistence but did decrease well-being.

12. This was subtext to our initial interview, but Caprielle confirmed her agreement with this take when she read over an advance copy of the book.

13. As mentioned in the author's note at the start, Connor felt he'd already been so active in fairly public student-voice efforts in Kentucky that anonymizing his profile was unnecessary, so we left identifying details in as per his request.

14. This may be because I asked a lot of questions about the program Connor was in that took him halfway across the state to live on a university campus as a high school junior. As a parent, I'd like to believe I'd be supportive of an opportunity like this, but initially it would make me pretty nervous. So, I really wanted to understand how Connor and his parents had built such a trusting relationship.

15. Levine, Ready or Not, is an interesting book on this topic.

16. See Polaris, "Managing Expectations with Your Adolescent," for a concise explanation of the different kinds of expectations parents can have of their teens. See Kennedy, Good Inside, for a deeper dive into how to set good boundaries as a parent, a close cousin to good expectations.

17. Dr. Becky Kennedy has a great TED Talk on repairing relationships after a rupture that you can find in video and audio versions with a web search; she also talks about it in her book, Good Inside (Kennedy 2022, 51-60).

18. We use the phrase "experienced practitioners" rather than "experts" because we believe young people are experts themselves, and all their ideas are obviously the focus of this book. However, sometimes it's helpful to get ideas from people with experience working with a wide range of young people and adults, and that's who we turned to for these ideas, which are in call out boxes throughout the book. These ideas come from a mix of three people: Leorah Walsh, MD, is a child psychiatrist with over a decade of experience working with teens and parents to support youth mental health. Elizabeth Daly, MSEd, is an experienced coach and teacher of executive functioning and motivation. Jessica Koehler, PhD, focused her doctoral work on adolescent motivation after having been a high school teacher for a decade, and is an accredited youth coach who works with high school and college students.

19. Menéndez, *Stand and Deliver*; Weir, *Dead Poets Society*; Warchus, *Matilda*; Daniels, *Abbott Elementary*. The first two were both released in the '80s, whereas the latter two both came out in the last few years.

20. Cornelius-White, "Learner-Centered Teacher-Student Relationships." This meta-analysis of 119 studies on the subject of learner-centered teacher-student relationships found that these kinds of relationships were positively associated with student cognitive, affective, behavioral, and overall outcomes.

21. Search Institute, "The Developmental Relationships Framework." Anyone familiar with research on developmental relationships may spot connections here—there is decades of research indicating how essential it is for young people to have relationships with adults that express care, challenge growth, provide support, share power, and expand possibilities. So, it's no surprise that when students felt teachers were doing these things, they were engaged in their classes and were interested in learning—even when it was a subject they'd previously had no interest in at all.

22. U.S Department of Education, "About IDEA." 504s and IEPs are shorthand references to legal documents, formal records of student disabilities that lay out what kinds of accommodations are needed for them to be able to have the same access to success in the classroom as students without those disabilities. They can range across physical and cognitive needs, and different school districts vary in their willingness to support

students getting these formal supports. 504 refers to section 504 of the Rehabilitation Act of 1973, which applies to workplaces as well as schools. IEPs refers to Individualized Education Programs, unique to early childhood or school environments, tied to the Individuals with Disabilities Education Act (IDEA).

23. *The Daily Show with Trevor Noah*, "Protests in Hong Kong Turn Violent."

24. Anderson, "Synthesis of research on mastery learning;" Bunt, "How Does Mastery Learning;" Saphier, The Skillful Teacher. See Anderson for a summative academic explanation, Bunt for a layperson's brief explanation of this approach, and Saphier for a pedagogical guide.

25. A few students we spoke with were in dual-enrollment programs to finish out their high school experience, like Zimo and Connor, and both of them spoke positively of these experiences, which is shared elsewhere. However, Grace, Nina, and Layla were the only students we interviewed who were exclusively in post-secondary school when we spoke to them.

26. To learn more about this group, go to www.ksvt.org

27. Hughes, "What They Take with Them."

28. The Trustees of the University of Pennsylvania 2023, "Leonard Davis Institute." This program, called Summer Undergraduate Minority Research (SUMR), is dedicated to supporting 30–40 scholars of color from any national university, pairing them with one to two research mentors for the summer. Grace described it as "a very individualistic program where every scholar works on their own various research projects, and at the end of the summer, we present our findings."

29. For anyone unfamiliar with how the name of the country Niger is pronounced in Spanish, a quick google search will take you to an audio file. While that pronunciation bears more similarities to the N-word in English than the English pronunciation of the country Niger, it's still pretty obvious that the only reason kids would begin chanting this word at a Black student is if they wanted to harass that student in a way that would give them plausible deniability later.

30. Khazan, "These Teens Got Therapy." This is especially the case if teens don't opt into this kind of material and are instead assigned to it, as this study in Australia discovered when DBT was mandated for a thousand ninth-grade public school students.

31. This hints at one of the conflicts that we struggled with most in looking at different school models. Seeing how much meaningful choice made a difference to students' experience makes opt-in programs like Ian's and Maria's very appealing to advocate for. However, any system that has the right to shunt the "least desirable" students to a "least desirable" school is likely to increase economic and racial divides that are already so gaping in our society.

32. Western Kentucky University, "The Gatton Academy of Mathematics and Science"

33. Hugh O'Brien Youth Leadership, "Leaders Built Here."

34. GripTape, "GripTape Challenge."

35. DeWitt, "To Have a Bigger Impact."

36. Part of what's going on likely is actual inattention sometimes—we talk about the effects, from adults' and students' perspectives, of contemporary media (especially social media) on everyone's abilities to pay attention, feel engaged, and feel connected in a separate chapter—but that's not the only factor at play, and when adults assume inattention is at the root of young people's confusion, we tacitly reinforce any growing beliefs that they shouldn't bother trying to learn the skill or topic at hand.

37. Tordoff, "Mental Health Outcomes." Tuesday was incredibly lucky that the physical bullying he experienced didn't lead to even worse consequences; for many trans students, the outcomes are far worse. Trans students who are not welcomed in their communities and by their families are significantly more likely to attempt suicide, and those who receive gender-affirming care as teens have far better outcomes.

38. Obviously we wouldn't be writing this book if we didn't think it was meaningful for parents and other invested adults to get involved in how education works and what's happening inside the school building. But there's a difference, to us, between parents who jump in on behalf of their children to make their school experience easier versus those who advocate for students to have real agency in school policies, curriculum, and so on.

39. Here we're deliberately using the terms Ariya used to describe herself, since she told us she was biracial when we asked how she wanted to be described in the book, and then said, "I'm Black and Puerto Rican." Though the US Census (Census Bureau, 2022) defines Latine/Hispanic as an ethnicity and not a race, many Latines view that status as both race

and ethnicity, so we always opt to describe people how they describe themselves.

40. Though Ariya didn't bring it up, most sources describe Fred Hampton's death as assassination, indicating he was drugged and unable to fire on the agents in the raid, which makes the framing of this incident in the way her teacher described it seem not just overly simplified, as Ariya called it, but also factually inaccurate.

41. Dweck, *Mindset*. See also Kaufman, "Growth Mindset Theory," for important caveats about the traditional approach to growth mindset in education, including the importance of knowing when to persist versus when not to, as well as the importance of a "personal growth mindset."

42. Mekouar, "Most of 2030's Jobs."

43. Damon, The Path to Purpose. This book offers an in-depth look at the impact purpose (long-term goals that are "of consequence beyond the self") can have on young people's well-being, and ideas for parents on how to support its development.

44. Fiery, "My ADHD Teen Has No Plans After High School!" This piece illustrates how goal-directedness can feel especially challenging for parents of young people with executive function disorders.

45. Ben-Shahar, Happier; Wilding, "Why Reaching Your Goals." These pieces (the second is a short article on Forbes that discusses Shahar's book), illustrate how, due to the effects of "arrival fallacy," actually reaching major goals you have worked towards for a long time can be deflating rather than enlivening—it's the act of making progress towards goals that correlates with well-being more so than goal attainment. That means it's also important to learn to value the process of goal-pursuit and stay grounded in a larger mission that underlies your goals rather than simply the goals themselves.

46. Coutinho, "The Relationship Between Goals" (39-47); Massey, "Adolescent Goal Content" (421-460); Pychyl, "Goal Progress and Happiness." The first two are academic texts with a thorough analysis of all elements, Pychyl's piece is a more lay-person friendly article on just the happiness element of goal pursuit.

47. The Search Institute, "Expand Possibilities." This is a thoughtful and accessible blog post on the details of what this can look like that we recommend reading if you're looking for more ideas.

48. Grant, *Hidden Potential*. Here Grant, renowned author and professor at Wharton, provides a salient example of what we're talking about. He tells a story about how he developed a goal to become a diver after being pushed out of his video game comfort zone by his mom, who had insisted he get out of the house and took him to a nearby pool to get him away from his console. He saw someone diving and became fascinated, and it sparked a curiosity that later developed into a goal. If his mom had directly pushed a goal on him, it probably would have backfired, but being prompted to get out of his comfort zone and see new things allowed a new interest to emerge that blossomed into a goal that prompted him to practice until he became a strong diver.

49. Horn, "Is Algebra Really Necessary?" Only about 11% of jobs involve work that require the use and understanding of concepts from Algebra 2. While only some states maintain this as a graduation requirement, it still stands as an example of irrelevance that can be preserved in requirements if we don't pause to assess why we're requiring what we're requiring. If those in school struggle to articulate why something is a requirement in a way that makes its value apparent to students, then perhaps instead of trying to figure out how to explain it we should be figuring out how to help students change it.

50. Premier Health, "Screen Addiction Affects." There is plenty written on this, but this is a short, parent-friendly article.

51. Choi, "Examining the Relationship," (1-7). This study found screen use not for work or school related purposes significantly correlated with decreased academic motivation for Chinese students.

52. Prinstein, "Written Testimony of Mitch Prinstein."

53. Prinstein, "Written Testimony," (14).

54. Prinstein, "Written Testimony," (15).

55. Prinstein, "Written Testimony," (6-7).

56. Prinstein, "Written Testimony," (7).

57. Prinstein, Written Testimony, 13-14

58. It's worth noting that what Caprielle witnessed in her school could be unusual, if the results of the recurring national survey on youth behavior are

accurate. They indicate a steady decline in self-reported sexual intercourse, sexual partners, and alcohol use. This means there is some conflict, potentially, between what Caprielle witnessed, what studies Prinstein cites are reporting about the risks of seeing risky behavior approved on the internet, and what the Youth Risk Behavior Survey found in results that came out shortly before COVID lockdowns. See Lehman, "Fewer American High Schoolers Having Sex," for a summary of those survey results.

59. Prinstein, Written Testimony

60. Ward, "Brain Drain."

61. Galla, "Rebel With a Cause."

62. American Psychological Association, "How Much is Too Much."

63. Sun, "The Effects of Online Game."

64. Navarro, "The Teenager Leading the Smartphone Liberation Movement."

65. See the clear and succinct Wikipedia summary on the history of this phrase, which was first used in Central European politics in the 1500s in its Latin form: Nihil de nobis, sine nobis (Wikipedia 2023).

66. Marken, "K-12 Workers Have Highest Burnout Rate in U.S.;" Jotkoff, "NEA Survey." Both these review recent major surveys (from Gallup and NEA respectively) show major burnout post-COVID, exacerbated by the staffing crisis created by so many teachers and other school staff leaving the field, which only increases the strain on those remaining.

67. If you want to go deeper with this line of questioning, we recommend checking out Nonviolent Communication, where there's a powerful activity focused on this idea (Rosenberg 2015, 136-7).

68. And because we wanted to make sure no interviewee felt their words were misinterpreted, we also invited all interviewees to read the complete draft of this book and flag any questions or concerns to us. About half our interviewees took us up on this offer. This approach blends principles of journalism with principles of youth participatory action research (YPAR) and modern ethnography research methods.

69. We're being deliberately vague about the grade he was in, and the name of the state test, in order to preserve Ian's privacy.

Bibliography

Ackerman, Courtney E., and Maike Neuhaus. 2018. "Self Determination Theory and How It Explains Motivation." PositivePsychology. com. https://positivepsychology.com/self-determination-theory/.

American Psychological Association. 2023. "How Much is Too Much Social Media Use: A Q&A with Mitch Prinstein, PhD." American Psychological Association. https://www.apa.org/topics/social-media-internet/social-media-literacy-teens.

Anderson, Stephen A. 1994. "Synthesis of Research on Mastery Learning," Information Analyses. ERIC. https://eric.ed.gov/?id=ED382567.

Bandura, Albert. 1989. "Human Agency in Social Cognitive Theory." *American psychologist* 44 (9): 1175.

Ben-Shahar, Tal. 2007. *Happier: Learn the Secrets to Daily Joy and Lasting Fulfillment.* N.p.: McGraw-Hill Education.

Bunt, Alexander. 2021. "How Does Mastery Learning Compare with Performance-Oriented Learning, and Why Should Teachers Care?" LinkedIn. https://www.linkedin.com/pulse/how-does-mastery-learning-compare-why-should-teachers-alexander-bunt/.

Census Bureau. 2022. "About the Topic of Race." Census Bureau. https://www.census.gov/topics/population/race/about.html.

Choi, Jaiyoun, and Jason I. Chen. 2022. "Examining the Relationship between Screen Time and Achievement Motivation in an Adolescent Population." *Journal of Emerging Investigators* 5 (June): 1-7. https://doi.org/10.59720/21-187.

Cornelius-White, Jeffrey. 2007. "Learner-Centered Teacher-Student Relationships Are Effective: A Meta-Analysis." *Review of Educational Research* 77, no. 1 (March): 113-143. http://www.jstor.org/stable/4624889.

Coutinho, Savia A. 2007. "The Relationship Between Goals, Metacognition, and Academic Success." *Educate~* 7 (1): 39-47.

The Daily Show with Trevor Noah. 2019. Season 4, episode 17, "Protests in Hong Kong Turn Violent." Featuring Trevor Noah. Comedy Central UK. Aired November 20, 2019. https://www.youtube.com/watch?v=zzYmcKAMfJM.

Damon, William. 2009. *The Path to Purpose: How Young People Find Their Calling in Life.* N.p.: Free Press.

Daniels, L., executive producer. 2021. *Abbott Elementary.* ABC Studios.

Deci, E. L., R. Koestner, and R. M. Ryan. 1999. "A Meta-Analytic Review of Experiments Examining the Effects of Extrinsic Rewards on Intrinsic Motivation." *Psychological Bulletin* 125 (6): 627-700. 10.1037/0033-2909.125.6.627.

DeWitt, Peter. 2022. "To Have a Bigger Impact, Here's What You Should Stop Doing in Your Classroom or School (Opinion)." Education Week. https://www.edweek.org/leadership/opinion-to-have-a-bigger-impact-heres-what-you-should-stop-doing-in-your-classroom-or-school/2022/12.

Dweck, Carol S. 2017. *Mindset.* 6th ed. N.p.: Robinson.

Ebbert, A. M., N. L. Kumar, and S. S. Luthar. 2019. "Complexities in Adjustment Patterns among the 'Best and the Brightest': Risk and Resilience in the Context of High Achieving Schools." *Research in Human Development* 16:21-34.

Fiery, Rick. 2023. "My ADHD Teen Has No Plans After High School!" ADDitude. https://www.additudemag.com/adhd-teen-plans-after-high-school/.

Galla, Brian. 2021. "Rebel With a Cause." Character Lab. https://characterlab.org/tips-of-the-week/rebel-with-a-cause/.

Grant, Adam. 2023. *Hidden Potential: The Science of Achieving Greater Things*. N.p.: Penguin Publishing Group.

GripTape. 2023. "GripTape Challenge." GripTape Challenge - Learn How and What You Want. https://www.griptape.org/.

Hodges, Tim. 2018. "School Engagement Is More Than Just Talk." Gallup. https://www.gallup.com/education/244022/school-engagement-talk.aspx.

Horn, Michael B. 2020. "Is Algebra Really Necessary?" EdSurge. https://www.edsurge.com/news/2020-03-10-is-algebra-really-necessary.

Howard, Joshua L., Julien Bureau, Frederic Guay, Jane X. Chong, and Richard M. Ryan. 2021. "Student Motivation and Associated Outcomes: A Meta-Analysis From Self-Determination Theory." *Perspectives on psychological science: A journal of the Association for Psychological Science* 16 (6): 1300-1323. 10.1177/1745691620966789.

Hughes, Bradley, Paula Gillespie, and Harvey Kail. 2010. "What They Take with Them: Findings from the Peer Writing Tutor Alumni Research Project." *The Writing Center Journal* 30 (2): 12-46. http://www.jstor.org/stable/43442343.

Hugh O'Brien Youth Leadership. 2023. "Leaders Built Here." HOBY Youth Leadership. https://hoby.org/.

Jotkoff, Eric. 2022. "NEA survey: Massive Staff Shortages in Schools Leading to Educator Burnout; Alarming Number of Educators Indicating They Plan to Leave Profession | NEA." National Education Association. https://www.nea.org/about-nea/media-center/press-releases/nea-survey-massive-staff-shortages-schools-leading-educator-burnout-alarming-number-educators.

Kaufman, Scott B. 2023. "Growth Mindset Theory: What's the Actual Evidence?" Beautiful Minds Newsletter. https://www.beautifulminds-newsletter.com/p/growth-mindset-theory-whats-the-actual?utm_campaign=post&utm_medium=web.

Kennedy, Becky. 2022. *Good Inside: A Guide to Becoming the Parent You Want to Be*. N.p.: HARPER WAVE.

Khazan, Olga. 2023. "These Teens Got Therapy. Then They Got Worse." *The Atlantic*, (Nov). https://www.theatlantic.com/ideas/archive/2023/11/teen-mental-health-dbt/675895/.

Lehman, Charles F. 2020. "Fewer American High Schoolers Having Sex Than Ever Before." Institute for Family Studies. https://ifstudies.org/blog/fewer-american-high-schoolers-having-sex-than-ever-before.

Levine, Madeline. 2020. *Ready Or Not: Preparing Our Kids to Thrive in an Uncertain and Rapidly Changing World*. N.p.: HarperCollins Publishers.

Li, Pamela. 2023. "Extrinsic Motivation: How Many Different Types Are There? (Examples)." Parenting For Brain. https://www.parentingforbrain.com/extrinsic-motivation/.

Luthar, S. S., N. L. Kumar, and N. Zillmer. 2020. "High-Achieving Schools Connote Risks for Adolescents: Problems Documented, Processes Implicated, and Directions for Interventions." *American Psychologist* 75:983-995.

Lythcott-Haims, Julie. 2015. *How to Raise an Adult: Break Free of the Overparenting Trap and Prepare Your Kid for Success*. N.p.: Henry Holt and Company.

Marken, Stephanie, and Sangeeta Agrawal. 2022. "K-12 Workers Have Highest Burnout Rate in U.S." Gallup News. https://news.gallup.com/poll/393500/workers-highest-burnout-rate.aspx.

Massey, Emma K., Winifred A. Gebhardt, and Nadia Garnefski. 2008. "Adolescent Goal Content and Pursuit: A Review of the Literature from the Past 16 Years." *Developmental Review* 28 (4): 421-460. https://doi.org/10.1016/j.dr.2008.03.002.

Mekouar, Dora. 2019. "Most of 2030's Jobs Haven't Been Invented Yet." VOA News. https://www.voanews.com/a/most-of-2030-s-jobs-haven-t-been-invented-yet/4778002.html.

Menéndez, Ramón, dir. 1988. *Stand and Deliver*. Warner Bros. Pictures.

Natanson, Hannah, Clara E. Morse, Anu Narayanswamy, and
Christina Brause. 2022. "These 64 Education Laws are Now
Part of America's Culture War." *The Washington Post*, October 18,
2022. https://www.washingtonpost.com/education/2022/10/18/
education-laws-culture-war/.

Navarro, Lulu G. 2023. "Opinion | The Teenager Leading the
Smartphone Liberation Movement." *The New York Times*,
February 2, 2023. https://www.nytimes.com/2023/02/02/
opinion/teen-luddite-smartphones.html.

Pinquart, Martin. 2016. "Associations of Parenting Styles and
Dimensions with Academic Achievement in Children and
Adolescents: A Meta-Analysis." *Educational Psychology Review*
28:475 - 493. https://doi.org/10.1007/s10648-015-9338-y.

Polaris Teen Center. 2019. "How to Manage the Expectations of
Your Adolescent." Polaris Teen Center. https://polaristeen.com/
articles/managing-expectations-with-teens/.

Premier Health. 2023. "Screen Addiction Affects Physical and
Mental Health." Premier Health. https://www.premierhealth.
com/your-health/articles/health-topics/screen-addiction-
affects-physical-and-mental-health.

Prinstein, Mitch. 2023. "Written Testimony of Mitch Prinstein,
PhD, ABPP, Chief Science Officer, American Psychological
Association, Protecting Our Children Online, Before the U.S.
Senate Committee on Judiciary." APA.org. Testimony. https://
www.apaservices.org/advocacy/news/testimony-prinstein-
protecting-children-online.pdf.

Pychyl, Timothy A. 2008. "Goal Progress and Happiness." Psychology
Today. https://www.psychologytoday.com/us/blog/dont-delay/
200806/goal-progress-and-happiness.

Reinicke, Carmen. 2022. "Florida Just Became the Largest State
to Mandate Personal Finance Education in High School."
CNBC, March 23, 2022. https://www.cnbc.com/2022/03/23/

florida-becomes-largest-state-to-mandate-personal-finance-
education-.html.

Rosenberg, Marshall B. 2015. *Nonviolent Communication: A Language
of Life: Life-Changing Tools for Healthy Relationships*. 3rd ed. USA:
PuddleDancer Press.

Ryan, R. M., and E. L. Deci. 2000. "Self-Determination Theory and
the Facilitation of Intrinsic Motivation, Social Development,
and Well-being." *The American Psychologist* 55 (1): 68-78. 10.1037//
0003-066x.55.1.68.

Saphier, Jon, Mary A. Haley-Speca, and Robert R. Gower. 2017.
*The Skillful Teacher: The Comprehensive Resource for Improving Teaching
and Learning*. 7th ed. N.p.: Research for Better Teaching,
Incorporated.

Search Institute. 2018. "The Developmental Relationships Framework."
Search Institute. https://www.search-institute.org/wp-content/
uploads/2018/05/Developmental-Relationships-Framework_
English.pdf.

Search Institute. 2018. "Expand Possibilities: Connections that Help
Kids Reach Their Potential." Search Institute Blog. https://blog.
searchinstitute.org/expand-possibilities.

Sun, Rui-Qi, Guo-Fang Sun, and Jian-Hong Ye. 2023. "The Effects
of Online Game Addiction on Reduced Academic Achievement
Motivation among Chinese College Students: The Mediating
Role of Learning Engagement." *Frontiers in Psychology* 14 (July).
10.3389/fpsyg.2023.1185353.

Tordoff, Diana, Jonathon Wanta, Arin Collin, Cesalie Stepney,
David J. Inwards-Breland, and Kym Ahrens. 2022. "Mental
Health Outcomes in Transgender and Nonbinary Youths
Receiving Gender-Affirming Care." *JAMA Network Open* 5 (2).
doi:10.1001/jamanetworkopen.2022.0978.

The Trustees of the University of Pennsylvania. 2023. "Leonard
Davis Institute Summer Undergraduate Minority Research

Institute | Penn CURF." Penn CURF. https://curf.upenn.edu/
content/leonard-davis-institute-summer-undergraduate-
minority-research-institute.

U.S. Department of Education. n.d. "About IDEA - Individuals
with Disabilities Education Act." U.S. Department of Education.
https://sites.ed.gov/idea/about-idea/.

Wallace, Jennifer B. 2023. *Never Enough: When Achievement Culture
Becomes Toxic-and What We Can Do About It*. N.p.: Penguin
Publishing Group.

Warchus, Matthew, dir. 2022. *Roald Dahl's Matilda the Musical*. Tristart
Pictures, Working Title Films, and The Roald Dahl Story Company.

Ward, Adrian F., Kristen Duke, Ayelet Gneezy, and Maarten W.
Bos. 2017. "Brain Drain: The Mere Presence of One's Own
Smartphone Reduces Available Cognitive Capacity." *Journal of
the Association for Consumer Research* 2, no. 2 (April). https://doi.
org/10.1086/691462.

Weir, Peter, dir. 1989. *Dead Poets Society*. Touchstone Pictures.

Western Kentucky University. 2022. "The Gatton Academy of
Mathematics and Science." Western Kentucky University.
https://www.wku.edu/academy/.

Wikipedia. 2023. "Nothing About Us Without Us." Wikipedia.
https://en.wikipedia.org/wiki/Nothing_about_us_without_us.

Wilding, Melody. 2023. "Why Reaching Your Goals Can Surprisingly
Make You Less Happy." Forbes. https://www.forbes.com/sites/
melodywilding/2016/08/22/why-reaching-your-goals-can-
surprisingly-make-you-less-happy/?sh=199d09deb880.

Acknowledgments

First and foremost, we want to thank all the young people, parents, and educators who have talked with us about their experiences, disappointments, and dreams for high school and college. Your stories inspired us, and we hope they will help readers of this book feel inspired, too.

We also want to thank Dr. Leorah Walsh, Dr. Jessica Koehler, and Elizabeth Daly for lending their expertise and feedback. Leorah, your early feedback came at just the right moment to keep the book moving forward, and your contributions to the ideas from experienced practitioners were invaluable. Thank you for turning your years of working with teens and families into succinct tips people can use. Jessica, your expertise in teen motivation and knowledge of all the secondary research helped us out of a bind many times—thank you for fact-checking our assertions about what the research shows about how teen motivation really works. Elizabeth, thank you for sharing the story from your classroom of the students who were asking you to please help them figure out how to feel motivated in school—you not only sparked the idea for this book by doing so but then also added useful insight from your time working with college and high school students to boot. Without all three of you, this book likely would not exist, so thank you!

Finally, to everyone at Atmosphere, thank you for helping to bring this book to life. To Tammy for pushing a major revision that was painful but necessary, to Alex for connecting us to the right people, to the art team for an amazing book cover, and to everyone who helped with proofreading, interior design, and production. You all have been a delight to work with, and we appreciate you.

From Grace: I want to thank my family, who encouraged me to pursue projects such as this. To my father, who supported me throughout my childhood as I navigated my complex identities and my education, and to my mother, who is supporting me as I navigate my adult life and new independence. To my high school teachers who first showed me what it meant to be valued and encouraged me to pursue my wildest dreams, even if it was unheard of at the time.

From Becca: I also want to specifically thank my family, who supported me in hiding out at my computer every weekend morning, working on this book until it was done. Mark, you provided so many helpful edits, plus useful pointers on AP style. Ryan and Jack, you helped me spot when things were getting boring and (mostly) tolerated me being unavailable to hang out and "do more fun stuff out of the house" when I was in the throes of writing and revising. I hope listening thoughtfully to all the wonderful young people who participated in our interviews helps me continue to listen to you all with as much curiosity and care and that we continue to work together to find ways to make school a more engaging place for you to learn and grow.

About Atmosphere Press

Founded in 2015, Atmosphere Press was built on the principles of Honesty, Transparency, Professionalism, Kindness, and Making Your Book Awesome. As an ethical and author-friendly hybrid press, we stay true to that founding mission today.

If you're a reader, enter our giveaway for a free book here:

SCAN TO ENTER
BOOK GIVEAWAY

If you're a writer, submit your manuscript for consideration here:

SCAN TO SUBMIT
MANUSCRIPT

And always feel free to visit Atmosphere Press and our authors online at atmospherepress.com. See you there soon!

About the Authors

REBECCA BLOCK has spent two decades working with students in various roles—first as an academic tutor after finishing her undergraduate degree, then as a Graduate Teaching Assistant and eventually as a full Professor teaching writing classes to undergraduate students, and most recently as a researcher and designer in nonprofits that work with K-12 schools. She's also the co-founder of Phare, LLC, an organization that supports teens, parents, and high schools through coaching and training, and the parent of two lively sons who patiently read early chapters of this book and gave feedback about how to cut all the "boring parts." Additionally, in the spirit of the same openness displayed by the interviewees in this book, she thinks it's important to name that she identifies as a neuroatypical, middle-aged, White woman who grew up in Kentucky, where she predominantly attended public suburban schools, and has since lived in Florida and Pennsylvania (the state she currently calls home).

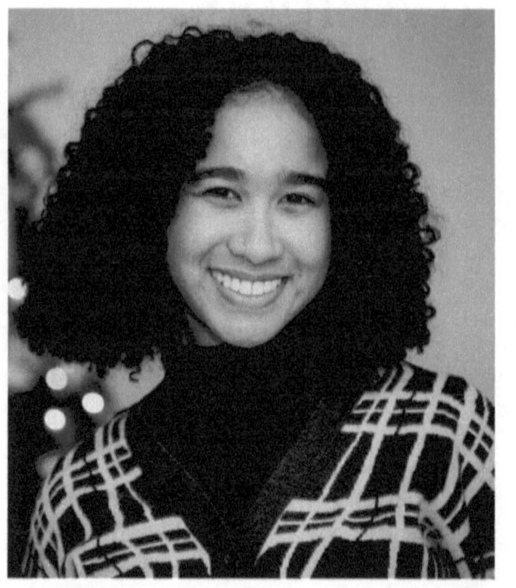 **GRACE EDWARDS,** a native-born "Marylander," is currently pursuing her undergraduate degree at the University of Pennsylvania in a Bachelor of Arts in Health and Societies, with a concentration in Race, Gender, and Health, and minoring in Journalism. In university, she's involved with the Pan-Asian American Community House (PAACH), Restorative Practices @ Penn, and volunteers with the unhoused community. After her undergraduate studies, she is hoping to pursue a career in the medical and healthcare field. As a budding young professional, she hopes to continue storytelling through long-form content and to continue writing about how people socialize, relate, and feel kinship with each other, despite their more obvious external differences. Ultimately, she is hoping to bridge these two interests in the practice of medicine and health.

www.ingramcontent.com/pod-product-compliance
Lightning Source LLC
Chambersburg PA
CBHW021342150726
47989CB00005B/2069